Florence Lin's
Chinese
One-Dish Meals

Florence Lin's Chinese One-Dish Meals

FLORENCE LIN

GRAMERCY PUBLISHING COMPANY
New York

To my daughters
Flora and Kay

This 1982 edition is published by Gramercy Publishers Company
distributed by Crown Publishers, Inc., by arrangement with
Hawthorn Properties (E.P. Dutton, Inc.)

Manufactured in the United States of America

Library of Congress Cataloging in Publication Data

ISBN: 0-517-386941

h g f e d c b a

Contents

Preface

As a cooking teacher, it has been my ambition over the last ten years to introduce authentic Chinese food to the American public. In order to reproduce an authentic food experience with success and reward, it is necessary first to learn to taste the food carefully, observing both the natural characteristics and the flavors of the ingredients, and then to learn the principles behind the cooking.

Chinese cooking is creative cooking. You do not have to buy exotic ingredients or spend hours preparing them. On the contrary, Chinese cooking can be inexpensive, simple, and quick. Ingredients are often very flexible. Recipes in cookbooks are only sample combinations of types of foods that can be put together; there is no reason for not substituting ingredients if they are handy, providing that the cook knows how to imagine different taste combinations. While changing an ingredient in a recipe does change the flavor of the dish, the final result can still taste good, and you will thereby be adding variation to your meals. For instance, while broccoli and asparagus are not vegetables indigenous to China, they are often used in the United States as substitutes for Chinese vegetables, both in the home and in Chinese restaurants. The preference for one ingredient over another is only a matter of taste. You may be—and should be—courageously flexible and creative in trying new combinations. This is how new dishes are made.

Florence Lin's
Chinese
One-Dish Meals

The Chinese Way of Cooking and Eating

What makes Chinese cooking Chinese? The simple and expected answer is that Chinese food is prepared in the Chinese way—that it is cooked and seasoned using special techniques and is prepared with special ingredients. This is of course true, but there is also a Chinese way of eating, which is equally basic to Chinese cooking.

Let us first consider the Chinese way of preparing food. Throughout China, with its many distinct regions and despite its many different styles of cooking, one of the common characteristics is the method of preparation—the cutting and the seasoning prior to cooking. Also common to all regions are the many cooking methods, such as stir-frying, steaming, and red-cooking, and, less familiar to Westerners, cooking with the firepot, the use of steamed *tien hsin*, and the serving of cold dishes that are made with cooked or partially cooked ingredients and are served along with hot foods. What does differ from region to region in China is the kind of ingredients and seasonings used—the vegetables, meat and seafood, herbs and spices, and sauces, which vary with each locality and according to their availability.

Here in the United States, typical Chinese ingredients are not always available. But this does not mean that you cannot cook in the Chinese fashion. The only Chinese ingredient that you absolutely need is soy sauce, and with the ingredients available to you, you will be able to cook an authentic Chinese meal from the recipes in this book.

However, there is a lesser known but no less intrinsic aspect of Chinese cooking, and that is the Chinese way of eating. Traditionally, there are three components to each meal: starch, vegetable, and meat. The starch is the primary and central part of the meal; it is typically rice in the South (cooked plain) and wheat products in the North. Vegetables, including soybeans and soybean products, are the major secondary foods, while meat, poultry, and fish are generally classified in daily meals as supplementary foods.

Along with this ample meal structure goes a simplified serving style. In a family-style meal, food is not served individually on a plate. Rather, each person is given a bowl of plain rice into which, during the course of the meal, he serves himself from the vegetables and meat placed at the center of the table. In this way, one can gauge one's own consumption according to one's individual appetite. Generally, vegetables and meats are cooked with more concentrated flavors than in Western cuisines in order that the meat can be eaten with a mouthful of rice. One usually alternates the eating of vegetables and meat with rice in between to clean the palate.

This has led to a simplified style of eating, the one-dish meal. In such a dish the meat and vegetables are combined at one time, in one cooking step, in order to provide a main dish, which can be accompanied by a simple salad or soup. Thus, the cooking and planning of the meal is greatly simplified. The concept is not a new one—in China the one-dish meal is served on passenger trains and is known as the "train meal." And in the United States, small rice shops regularly serve the one-dish meal over plain rice and with a tall glass of hot tea. Today, Chinese families everywhere frequently prepare the one-dish meal. It is excellent not only for everyday meals for working families but even as the basis of a special-occasion company meal or as part of a gourmet feast. Its ease of preparation makes it particularly appropriate for the contemporary life-style.

Planning Chinese Dinners with One-Dish Meals

Chinese food, and one-dish cooking in particular, has a number of unexpected assets. Not only is it good tasting but it can be prepared quickly (thirty minutes for a meal composed of one Chinese dish and rice), and it is economical, nutritious, and filling. It can be superb fare for company or a special delight for everyday eating. The trick is in the planning.

Planning such meals involves wise shopping, proper storage, defrosting shortcuts, precooking, and special methods of reheating. For example, in shopping for vegetables and meats, one should be flexible in selecting what is available and fresh, vegetables and fruits especially. They taste the best when they are in season and are usually less expensive then as well. Proper storage is equally important. After foods are brought home from the store, regardless of how fresh they may be, they will become stale or wilted after three to four days of refrigeration if not properly wrapped. Vegetables will stay fresh longer if doubly wrapped in a brown bag inside a sealed plastic one before being stored in the refrigerator. In this way, excess droplets of water are absorbed by the brown paper, but at the same time the moisture keeps the vegetables from wilting. However, if you have kept the vegetables too long or if you should fail to store them properly, you can revive them by soaking them in lukewarm water for about an hour before washing with cold water. They will taste almost as good as fresh ones.

Similarly, a little preplanning when storing meat can be a real time-saver. Before freezing, simply divide the meat into portion sizes that recipes normally call for. For example, a whole flank steak can be divided into thirds (roughly ¾ pound each) before freezing, since one portion will be sufficient for each recipe. Each portion can be separately wrapped and frozen, to be defrosted on an as-needed basis.

Defrosting offers another opportunity to simplify Chinese cooking. If the meat or vegetables to be used in an evening's meal is frozen, remove it from the freezer the night or morning before and let it thaw slowly in the refrigerator. Usually this means that the food will be partially frozen when it is time to prepare the meal, which will make slicing easier. Partially frozen meats and many vegetables can also be sliced successfully in a food processor.

A number of Chinese foods can be prepared ahead of time. Stewed (braised) and slow-cooked foods, which are rarely included in restaurant menus, are very good hot and are easily reheated, but they are also good when eaten cold.

Rice can also be prepared ahead of time. In fact, it is time and labor saving to always prepare more than is needed for one meal, since rice is easily stored in the refrigerator and reheated. Simply transfer cooled leftover rice to a tightly covered container, after which it can be kept in the refrigerator for a week to ten days without spoiling. Although cooked rice becomes hard when stored in the refrigerator, it can be made soft again by steaming, and such reheating does not affect its texture significantly. In fact, you can hardly differentiate between it and freshly cooked rice.

Through the intelligent use of freezing, defrosting, and reheating techniques, the working person can regularly have a hot meal just a short time after returning home from a day's work. Just scoop out a portion of cold cooked rice from the refrigerator and put it into a porcelain or glass bowl. Sprinkle some water over the rice. Set the bowl with the rice in a steamer or in a pan with some water. Cover and steam for fifteen minutes. The rice will be piping hot and can be eaten from the same hot bowl, along with meats and vegetables that were also prepared in advance or with a cold main dish. By cooking in this manner, you will be getting a hot meal, yet only a few dishes are used. Hence, there are fewer dishes to be washed, and best of all, there is no pot to be cleaned.

Taking Advantage of the Versatility of Foods

A one-dish meal that consists of a stir-fried dish offers the potential to cope with unexpected dinner guests. For example, if you have only two pork chops, it might seem difficult and awkward to make four servings. But for a stir-fried dish, the food is cut into bite-size pieces, with the number of portions flexible. To stretch a stir-fried dish, either add more of the same vegetables or add one portion of some of the other vegetables suggested at the end of each recipe. If you wish to make a dish more elaborate, add fresh or dried mushrooms, bamboo shoots, or water chestnuts. It is also very common in China to add an egg dish of three or four scrambled eggs with scallions to the planned menu if there is an extra person for dinner. Finally, Szechuan Pickled Cabbage (page 135) and Spiced Pickled Cucumber (page 143) are handy vegetables to keep in the refrigerator; they add a refreshing touch to any dinner.

Planning a Dinner for Company

For company, red-cooked or stew-type dishes may be enlarged by cooking more than one recipe, but with stir-fried dishes it is better to cook more dishes of the same size. Furthermore, the only way to prepare good stir-fried dishes at home is to cook them in small portions; a double portion of a recipe is the largest workable quantity of food to be cooked by stir-frying. As a general rule, never stir-fry more than one pound of meat or fish at one time. This is because the home range does not give off enough heat to stir-fry large amounts of meat properly, and therefore the food will not cook well. Rather than being tender and juicy, meat will become chewy and dry, with a watery gravy.

Since stir-fried dishes always require last-minute cooking, a dinner should not include more than one or two of them. In planning a company meal, the menu should consist of dishes cooked by different methods. Generally, half a pound of meat is allocated for each person in a dinner party. If a host or hostess is planning a Chinese dinner with four dishes for eight persons, this does not necessarily mean that each dish should contain exactly one pound of meat. Be flexible. If one dish includes a three-pound chicken, the other two dishes might be a small steamed fish and a stir-fried meat and vegetable dish, while the fourth dish can be a salad of vegetables that can be cooked ahead of time and eaten cold.

For elaborate dinners use better cuts of meat and better quality fish, such as filet mignon instead of flank steak, fresh shrimp instead of frozen, hearts of vegetables instead of the entire plant, squabs or duck instead of chicken. Virginia ham, dried or fresh mushrooms, winter bamboo shoots, or fresh water chestnuts may be added to embellish and enhance the taste of a dish. But do not add these ingredients at random, for sometimes different flavors do not complement one another. In order to know what are good combinations, one must have eaten a lot of Chinese food. To help the person who does not have much experience with Chinese food, I have provided, at the end of each recipe in this book, suggestions as to what kinds of ingredients may be substituted or added to a dish. These suggestions are only a few of the many variations that can be made to a recipe, but it is a good guideline that any novice cook can follow without having to do any experimenting. In addition to the dinner, one or two hors d'oeuvres may be served, and fresh fruits flavored with a liqueur would be a good dessert. Some of the lighter Western desserts also go well with Chinese meals.

Variety—The Key to the Planning of Any Meal

In planning a meal you should consider not only the quality and quantity of foods, but also their variety of color, shape of cut, texture, and flavor.

Soy sauce is an essential seasoning liquid that plays the most important part in Chinese cooking in terms of both taste and color. However, if all the dishes in a meal are cooked with soy sauce, they will all be brown in color. Therefore, do use soy sauce discriminately. Above all, a connoisseur of Chinese food will never, never pour soy sauce over plain cooked rice unless the rest of the dinner is not palatable.

With the inclusion of different vegetables, meats, and fish, a dinner can be very colorful. For example, you might use green peas, orange carrots, white cauliflower, white fish fillet, pink shrimp, and so forth.

Cutting food into different shapes not only makes a meal more interesting but has a definite purpose as well. For slow-cooking methods, the vegetables should be cut into chunks, whereas for stir-frying, they must be cut into matchstick shreds or thin slices. This is because the shreds and thin slices cook quickly, which is desirable in stir-frying, while if you take the same finely cut foods and simmer them, they will fall apart.

The Chinese feel that the quality of crispness is very important to the pleasure of eating. However, if all the foods in a dish require a lot of chewing or if you are serving several dishes containing only foods that require a lot of chewing, your guests' jaws may get very tired. So, most of the food in a Chinese one-dish meal should have a tender, soft, or smooth texture, with perhaps one "crispy" food to highlight the rest. Similarly, although many people enjoy highly seasoned food with strong flavors, some mild and rather bland food should also be included in a well-planned dinner for contrast.

Stir-Fried Dishes

NAME OF DISH	NATURE OF DISH	PAGE
Niu Jou Sung Chopped Beef with Peas	Simple cooking, with or without exotic ingredients, and served in a lettuce leaf package.	38
Ch'ao Hsien Kan Pei Stir-Fried Fresh Scallops	This must be cooked with care to get the right delicate texture.	40
Mien Pao Hsia Jen Diced Shrimp with Croutons	The croutons will absorb some of the shrimp gravy, but they remain partially crispy.	43
Tan Chiao Pork Omelets with Celery Cabbage	Simplified small omelets that can be cooked ahead of time.	46
Huo T'ui Tsai Hua Cauliflower with Ham	A colorful dish with many vegetables that has a subtle ham flavor.	48
Ch'ao Lung Hsia Lobster with Meat Sauce	One lobster (1½ pounds) may be stretched into a delicious dish for a hearty meal for two persons.	50
Ch'ao Sheng Ts'ai Stir-Fried Romaine Lettuce	Quick stir-fried leaf vegetables with many variations; excellent in combination with red-cooked dishes.	52
Ch'ao Ts'ai Hua Stir-Fried Cauliflower	A group of stir-fried vegetable dishes that has less liquid than the ones with leafy vegetables. They are very good combined with stir-fried meat, fish, or seafood for one-dish meals.	54
Ch'ao Tou Chiao Stir-Fried Green Beans	This dish contains soy sauce and requires a longer cooking time. Therefore, it has a more concentrated flavor and is good with Plain Rice. Many variations.	56

Stir-frying, or *ch'ao*, is a uniquely Chinese cooking method. This quick-cooking method (which takes only a few minutes) produces delicious dishes. There are just a few basic steps, and they are common to almost all stir-fried dishes. First, a pan or wok is heated until very hot. Then, oil is added and heated up to just below the smoking point. Next, the precut ingredients (which are sometimes marinated) are added and quickly stirred, mixed, and seasoned. In certain dishes, some liquid is added at this stage, and the food is allowed to simmer, covered, for a couple of minutes. Or the food is cooked in its own juices. Finally, a mixture of cornstarch and water is frequently added to thicken the liquid.

Although, conceptually, stir-frying seems easy to learn, it is somewhat more difficult to master, due to the necessity for controlled heat and the quick action required in the seasoning and stirring steps. It is most important to have all ingredients set out beside the range before you start heating the pan; there's no time to look for ingredients or to cut food at the last minute. Following are some suggestions that, with practice, should be all that are needed to start a beginner on his or her way.

First, some hints regarding the stir-fry cooking process:

• Depending on the marinade and seasoning, stir-fried dishes can be either of two basic "colors." One kind is cooked with dark soy sauce and is called dark-cooking, and the other is cooked with light soy sauce or without soy sauce and is called light-cooking. The light is lighter in taste than the dark, but both can be spicy in flavor.

• If a stir-fried dish consists of both meat and vegetables, always cook the meat and vegetables separately, and then combine them. Or you can cook the vegetables first, seasoning with salt and sugar, and keep them hot in a 175° oven while you cook the meat. Then, just top the vegetables with the cooked meat. This gives a nice contrast of colors to the dish. One may serve such a dish without using the cornstarch-and-water thickening agent, thereby giving the dish a lighter and more refreshing taste.

• While stir-frying, one should always carefully watch the cooking of the food and not be afraid to adjust the heat if it seems either too high or too low for the ingredients. The food should not be overcooked, burned, or even browned, except in some dishes in which a "wok flavor," similar to a barbecue taste, is desired.

• If a dish is cooked but there is too much gravy in the pan, use a slotted spoon to extract the solids while you leave the gravy in the pan. Then, continue to cook and stir the gravy over high heat until the excess liquid has evaporated.

• For best results, it is better to limit the amount of food in the pan to under one pound. In fact, the smaller the quantity, the easier the stir-frying will be. Do not attempt to double a recipe; rather cook two separate batches. For the best-tasting results, stir-fried dishes should be served hot, immediately after being dished out of the pan.

Here are a number of suggestions regarding the ingredients used in stir-frying:

• Stir-fried foods are always cut into matchstick shreds, thin slices, dice, or small cubes. Never use big chunks of any food, even if the food is good to eat raw, because there will be no time for the seasoning to penetrate them.

• Beef can be aged in your own refrigerator. Simply lightly oil the meat, loosely cover it, place it in the refrigerator and turn it each day. After 3 to 4 days, the beef will be much more tender.

• If meat seems dry after cutting, add 1 to 2 tablespoons water and mix with your hand before adding the marinade. This makes the meat more juicy and gives it a fluffier texture.

• Stir-fried pork must always be cooked thoroughly. However, one must be careful *not* to overcook beef, chicken, fish, or seafood.

• The proportion of meat to vegetables is flexible in a stir-fried dish. However, in general, an everyday meal consists of less meat and more vegetables. This helps reduce food costs greatly while not sacrificing flavor. The dish usually has one vegetable that dominates in flavor, with other vegetables added to enhance the taste and texture. For example, green pepper is often a dominant vegetable in a dish. To one portion of peppers you might add one-quarter of that amount of mushrooms and bamboo shoots or water chestnuts to give the dish added taste and texture, and you might even add a small amount of blanched carrots to add color and texture. All the ingredients of a dish should be more or less uniform in cut and size; that is, the ingredients should all be shredded or all sliced and all the pieces should be of the same thickness in order that they all reach the same degree of doneness.

• In order to avoid a last-minute rush prior to serving a stir-fried dish, one can cut up the vegetables and season the meat ahead of time or even parboil or stir-fry the vegetables ahead of time and then add them to the meat during the last minutes of cooking.

• Frozen, but not canned, green vegetables may be substituted for fresh.

• Fresh meat may be frozen in small, flat packages. A flat portion such as this will partially defrost in 10 to 15 minutes and will be just soft enough to cut into thin slices or shreds or any other style. Then, allow the cut meat to defrost completely while the vegetables are being cleaned and cut. By the time the vegetables are cut, the meat will be defrosted enough to allow it to be marinated. All the preparations for a stir-fried dish may thus be completed several hours ahead of time, leaving only a few last minutes for the actual stir-frying.

• Before cooking, set all the cut-up ingredients in separate piles on a large plate. This makes it easier to slide them into the pan during cooking and minimizes cleanup, since the same plate can also be used for serving.

• Soy sauce is an important ingredient to most of the recipes in this book. I recommend the use of imported Chinese soy sauce (which contains less sugar and more salt than other varieties) and coarse salt. Adjust the saltiness to taste if you use anything other than that. Monosodium glutamate, which I use in some of the recipes, is a flavor enhancer. It is found naturally in almost all plants and in animal protein, with sugar beets, wheat, and corn the major sources. If you use a small amount, that is, ⅛ to ¼ teaspoon per recipe, you will probably have no side effects.

Leftover stir-fried dishes can also be successfully reheated as they are or used to create a totally new dish. Specifically:

- If you have to reheat a stir-fried dish, add only a small amount of water or broth and place over medium heat until just hot.
- If you have a microwave oven, you can reheat a stir-fried dish quickly and successfully, stirring once for a large plate of food.
- Never throw away leftover stir-fried dishes and especially not the gravy. Although only a few slices of meat with gravy may be left, they will be wonderful combined with the next meal's vegetables. Simply add them to the next day's vegetables near the end of the cooking time and cook until just heated through. This will give the vegetables a better flavor.
- Leftovers with a little gravy are good as an accompaniment for fried rice. Just follow the basic Fried Rice recipe (page 157), add the leftovers to the rice, and allow to heat through thoroughly before serving.
- If you do not have a wok, a 3-quart saucepan or skillet lined with a non-stick surface, such as Silver-Stone or Teflon, are good substitutes because they require less oil and less space for storage, and are easy to clean and handle.

Finally, in preparing a new dish, follow the basic recipe closely at first until you grasp the principle behind the cooking. Then you can be more flexible and creative in trying new combinations. Stir-fried dishes are not only easy and quick, they have a unique texture and flavor that make them well worth cooling and serving often.

Ch'ao Chu Jou Pien

STIR-FRIED PORK WITH PEPPERS

¾ pound boneless pork cutlets (bottom or hip loin)

Marinade:
   2 teaspoons cornstarch
   2 tablespoons cold water
   2 tablespoons soy sauce

   5 tablespoons peanut or corn oil
   6 large green peppers, cut into 1-inch pieces (about
      6 cups)
 1½ teaspoons salt
   ½ teaspoon sugar
   1 tablespoon dry sherry
   ½ tablespoon cornstarch combined with
      3 tablespoons water

If an ingredient in the basic recipe is not readily available, or if an exotic variation is desired, see the list at the end of the recipe.

Preparation:
Slice pork into 2 × 1 × ⅛-inch pieces (there should be about 1½ cups). Combine the sliced meat with the marinade ingredients, and, using your hand, mix well with the meat. The meat can be either cooked right away or covered and kept in the refrigerator for as long as overnight.

Cooking:
Heat a pan or wok over medium heat until very hot. Add 2 tablespoons of the oil, then stir-fry the peppers for 4 to 5 minutes. Add the salt and sugar. Mix well and transfer to a plate. Clean out the pan, then reheat until hot. Add the remaining 3 tablespoons oil. Mix the pork and marinade again and add to the pan. Stir-fry over high heat until the pork begins to separate into slices and the color of all the meat has changed. Sprinkle the sherry onto the pork. Add the peppers and stir and cook to heat through. Mix the cornstarch-and-water combination very well and slowly pour this into the pan; stir until the sauce thickens and a clear glaze coats the meat and vegetables. Serve hot with Plain Rice (pages 153-155).

Yield: 4 servings. If more servings are desired, or for a more substantial and elaborate meal, read the menu planning chapter, page 6.

Choice of meat and cutting style: After being trimmed, the meat may be partially frozen to facilitate slicing. Instead of pork cutlets you may use pork (center cut, fresh butt or ham), sliced; flank or shell steak, sliced against the grain; filet mignon, cubed or sliced with the grain; chicken breast, sliced with the grain; or veal cutlet, sliced with the grain.

Choice of vegetable and method of cooking: Instead of green peppers, you may use zucchini, asparagus, and celery, cut diagonally into ¼-inch slices; green beans, cut into 2-inch sections; broccoli and cauliflower, cut into flowerets with stems; cabbage, cut into 2 × 1-inch pieces. You may substitute 1½ cups of cut-up fresh mushrooms for 1½ cups of any of the above vegetables. To add color and texture, add 10 slices parboiled carrots. Some vegetables require a little water and longer cooking time; just add a few tablespoons water and cook the vegetable until it looks translucent but is still crisp.

The vegetables may be cooked and seasoned ahead of time and kept hot in a 175° oven while you cook the meat. Then top the vegetables with the cooked meat, omitting the cornstarch-and-water thickening agent.

Frozen or parboiled vegetables may be used. There is no need to stir-fry them separately. Add 1 more tablespoon oil to stir-fry the meat; then combine the vegetables and add 1 tablespoon soy sauce and ½ teaspoon sugar to the cornstarch-and-water thickening agent, then combine the vegetables.

Choice of exotic ingredients and seasonings: Sliced winter bamboo shoots, presoaked Chinese dried mushrooms, canned straw mushrooms, peeled fresh or canned water chestnuts, sliced bok choy, or snow pea pods may be used instead of green peppers. And you may add 2 teaspoons chopped fresh gingerroot and 1 clove chopped garlic to the hot oil before adding the raw meat.

Ch'ao Niu Jou Pien

STIR-FRIED ONION STEAK

¾ pound flank steak (about ⅓ whole steak, cut lengthwise)

Marinade:
1 tablespoon cornstarch
2 tablespoons cold water
2 tablespoons soy sauce

3 medium yellow onions
4 tablespoons peanut or corn oil

If an ingredient in the basic recipe is not readily available, or if an exotic variation is desired, see the list at the end of the recipe.

Preparation:
Cut a whole large flank steak lengthwise into three strips. Wrap two of the strips individually and store in the freezer for future use. Slice the third strip against the grain into ¼-inch-thick slices (there should be about 1½ cups). Combine the sliced meat with the marinade ingredients and, using your hand, mix well with the meat. The meat can be either cooked immediately or covered and kept in the refrigerator for up to 24 hours.

Cut off the ends of each onion. Remove and discard the outer skin layers. Cut onions into ½-inch wedges and separate the layers to make about 2 cups. Set aside.

Cooking:
Heat a pan or wok over medium heat until hot. Add 1 tablespoon of the oil. Add the onions and stir-fry in the hot oil for about 2 minutes. If the onions start to burn, sprinkle with some water. The onions should still be crisp. Remove from the pan and set aside. Reheat the pan and add the remaining 3 tablespoons oil. Mix the marinated meat again and add it to the oil, quickly stirring over high heat to separate the meat slices. Cook until the meat just turns color, then add the cooked onions. Stir to mix well and let it heat through. Do not overcook. Serve hot with Plain Rice (pages 153-155).

Yield: 4 servings. If more servings are desired, or for a more substantial and elaborate meal, read the menu planning section, page 6.

Choice of meat and cutting styles: After being trimmed, the meat may be partially frozen to facilitate slicing. Instead of flank steak you may use skirt, sirloin, or shell steak, sliced against the grain or cut into matchstick strips with the grain; filet mignon, sliced with the grain; or leg of lamb (lean and without gristle), sliced.

Choice of vegetables: When the meat is cut into matchstick strips, the onions should also be cut into strips. Or you may cut 2 cups leeks or scallions diagonally into ¼-inch sections.

Choice of seasonings: For a spicier flavor, add to the heated oil before cooking the *marinated meat:* 1 teaspoon crushed red pepper, or to taste; and 1 clove garlic, thinly sliced. For a more pungent flavor, make the following sauce, which is especially good with lamb and scallions:

½ teaspoon sugar
1 tablespoon soy sauce
1 tablespoon dry sherry
1 teaspoon distilled white vinegar
2 teaspoons sesame oil

Combine all ingredients and stir until well blended, then add to the cooked meat and vegetables just before the cooking is complete.

Ma Ku Chi Pien

STIR-FRIED CHICKEN WITH FRESH MUSHROOMS

This very popular dish is made without soy sauce and is commonly called Mu Goo Gai Pei.

1   *whole boneless chicken breast (about 6 ounces)*

Marinade:
   2   *teaspoons cornstarch*
   2   *tablespoons cold water*
   ½   *teaspoon salt*
   ¼   *teaspoon monosodium glutamate*

   2   *medium zucchini*
   ⅓   *pound fresh mushrooms*
   ¼   *cup thinly sliced parboiled carrots*
   4   *tablespoons peanut or corn oil*
   1   *tablespoon dry sherry*
   1   *teaspoon salt*
   ½   *tablespoon cornstarch combined with*
      3   *tablespoons water*

If an ingredient in the basic recipe is not readily available, or if an exotic variation is desired, see the list at the end of the recipe.

Preparation:
Slice the chicken with the grain into 2 × 1 × ⅛-inch pieces (there should be about 1 cup). Combine the sliced chicken with the marinade ingredients and, using your hand, mix well with the poultry. The

26

chicken can be either cooked right away or covered and kept in the refrigerator for up to 24 hours.

Cut the zucchini lengthwise into halves, then slice diagonally into ½-inch pieces (about 4 cups). Slice the mushrooms (about 2 cups) and set both vegetables on a large plate with the sliced parboiled carrots.

Cooking:
Heat a pan or wok over medium heat until it becomes very hot. Add 2 tablespoons of the oil, then add the chicken, and stir-fry to separate the slices. If the chicken seems to stick to the pan, add a little more oil. As soon as the chicken separates into slices, sprinkle it with the sherry, mix well, and transfer to a plate.

Reheat the pan, add the remaining 2 tablespoons oil, and stir-fry the zucchini, mushrooms, and carrots over medium-high heat for about 2 minutes. Add the salt and mix well. Add the cooked chicken. Stir to combine with the vegetables and to heat through. Mix the cornstarch-and-water combination very well and pour slowly into the pan, continuing to stir until the sauce thickens and a clear glaze coats the chicken and vegetables. Serve hot.

Yield: 4 servings. If more servings are desired, or for a more substantial and elaborate meal, read the menu planning chapter, page 6.

Choice of meat, fish, or seafood: Instead of chicken, you may use ½ pound veal cutlet, sliced with the grain; pork cutlet, sliced with the grain; fresh raw shrimp, shelled, deveined, and split in half if large (and instead of using water in the marinade, use ½ egg white); bay or sea scallops (if sea scallops, split in half; instead of using water in the marinade, use ½ egg white); fillet of sea bass, yellow pike, sole, and other fish of similar texture, cut into 2-inch squares (instead of using water in the marinade, use ½ egg white).

Choice of vegetables: You may use 4 cups asparagus, cut diagonally into ½-inch slices; celery, sliced with the grain, with leaves, outer layer, and veins removed; cucumber, peeled and sliced, with seeds removed; sliced canned mushrooms, bamboo shoots, or straw mushrooms; presoaked dried Chinese black mushrooms, peeled fresh or canned water chestnuts, fresh snow pea pods, or fresh green beans.

Kung Pao Chi Ting

CHICKEN WITH PEANUTS

4 chicken legs, boned and skinned

Marinade:
1 tablespoon cornstarch
2 tablespoons cold water
1 tablespoon soy sauce

2 teaspoons minced fresh gingerroot
1 clove garlic, minced
1 to 2 teaspoons crushed red pepper
½ cup skinless roasted peanuts, preferably unsalted
¼ cup peanut or corn oil

Sauce:
1 teaspoon sugar
1 teaspoon cornstarch
2 tablespoons soy sauce
1 tablespoon dry sherry
1 tablespoon cold water
1 teaspoon distilled white vinegar
1 teaspoon sesame or corn oil

If an ingredient in the basic recipe is not readily available, or if a variation is desired, see the list at the end of the recipe.

Preparation:
Cut the chicken into ½-inch cubes. (There should be about 1½ cups.) Combine the chicken cubes with the

marinade ingredients and, using your hand, mix well with the poultry. The chicken can be either cooked immediately or covered and kept in the refrigerator for up to 24 hours.

Prepare the gingerroot and garlic and set aside on a plate in separate piles, along with the crushed red pepper and the peanuts.

Cooking:
Heat a pan or wok over medium heat until it becomes very hot. Add the oil and stir-fry the chicken over medium-high heat for 2 to 3 minutes, or until the chicken cubes separate and all the pieces change color. Remove the chicken to a plate with a slotted spoon, leaving the excess oil in the pan.

Reheat the pan. Add the gingerroot and brown lightly, then add the garlic and crushed red pepper and fry for 10 seconds. Add the cooked chicken and stir-fry over high heat for 1 minute. Stir the sauce ingredients, making sure that the sugar and cornstarch are well mixed, and add the sauce to the chicken, continuing to stir over high heat until the sauce thickens and coats the chicken with a clear glaze. Add the peanuts and mix well. Serve hot with Plain Rice (pages 153-155) and, since this dish does not include vegetables, a stir-fried green vegetable dish or salad.

Yield: 4 servings. If more servings are desired, or for a more substantial and elaborate meal, read the menu planning chapter, page 6.

Choice of meat: Instead of chicken legs, you may use boneless, skinless chicken breast, cut into ½-inch cubes; or boneless pork, cut into thin slices.

Choice of vegetable: Instead of peanuts, you may use 1 large green pepper, cut into 1-inch cubes and parboiled for 2 minutes.

Choice of seasoning: Cut-up fresh hot pepper may be used instead of crushed red pepper.

Hua Niu

SLIPPERY BEEF

An unusual cooking procedure is used to give the beef a unique coating and texture. This is a typical Cantonese dish.

¾ pound boneless shell steak (strip steak)

Marinade:
1 egg white
2 tablespoons cornstarch
2 tablespoons soy sauce

3 medium tomatoes (about 1 pound)
3 tablespoons peanut or corn oil

Sauce:
1 teaspoon cornstarch
1 tablespoon cold water
1 teaspoon sugar
1½ tablespoons soy sauce
¼ teaspoon monosodium glutamate

If an ingredient in the basic recipe is not readily available, or if a variation is desired, see the list at the end of the recipe.

Preparation:
Slice the beef into 1½ × 1 × ¼-inch pieces (there should be 1½ cups). Place the beef in a mixing bowl. Add the egg white and cornstarch and, using your

hand, mix well with the meat. If the meat seems dry, add 1 tablespoon water. Add the soy sauce and mix some more. Keep the marinated meat in the refrigerator for 30 minutes, or as long as 24 hours.

Dip the tomatoes in boiling water for 5 seconds. Peel, then cut each into 6 or 8 wedges. Remove the seeds and set the tomatoes aside on a plate. Combine the sauce ingredients in a cup and set on the same plate.

In a large pot bring 1 quart water to a rolling boil. Add the marinated beef and stir gently to separate the pieces. The beef will now be 90 percent cooked. Remove from the heat and drain immediately. Cool in 1 quart cold water. Drain well again. The meat can sit for several hours at this stage.

Cooking:
Heat a pan or wok over medium heat until very hot. Add the oil. Then add the tomatoes and stir-fry for 1 minute. Turn heat to high and add the drained beef. Stir and mix. Add the sauce ingredients. Keep over high heat and stir gently until the sauce coats everything well. Serve hot with Plain Rice (pages 153-155).

Yield: 4 servings. If more servings are desired, or for a more substantial and elaborate meal, read the menu planning chapter, page 6.

Choice of meat: Sliced flank, sirloin steak, veal, pork, or chicken cutlet may be used instead of beef.

Choice of vegetables: Instead of tomatoes, you may use

2 cups parboiled onions, cut into 1-inch wedges, 2 cups parboiled broccoli or cauliflower, cut into flowerets, with stems about 2 inches long; or to give color and texture, ½ cup sliced parboiled carrots, sliced fresh or canned water chestnuts, or bamboo shoots may be added.

Choice of exotic ingredients and seasonings: You may add 1 teaspoon chopped fresh gingerroot to the hot oil before you cook the vegetables and meat (add more if young gingerroot is used). You may use 1 tablespoon oyster sauce in the sauce ingredients instead of the cornstarch and monosodium glutamate (but reduce the soy sauce to 1 tablespoon).

Mu Shu Jou

MU SHU PORK (SIMPLIFIED)

This northern Chinese egg dish is usually served with Mandarin Pancakes (page 172).

   ½ *pound pork cutlet*

Marinade:
- 1 *teaspoon cornstarch*
- 1 *tablespoon cold water*
- 1½ *tablespoons soy sauce*

- 2 *cups shredded cabbage*
- 2 *to 3 scallions*
- 4 *tablespoons peanut or corn oil*
- 3 *large eggs, broken into a bowl*
- 1½ *teaspoons salt*
- ¼ *teaspoon monosodium glutamate*
- 2 *teaspoons sesame or corn oil*

If an ingredient in the basic recipe is not readily available, or if a more authentic recipe is desired, see the list at the end of the recipe.

Preparation:
Cut the pork into paper-thin slices, then into matchstick strips 1½ to 2 inches long (there should be about 1 cup). Combine the pork slices with the marinade and, using your hand, mix well with the meat. Set aside.

Shred the cabbage into 2 × ⅛-inch strips to make 2 cups. Set on a large plate. Trim the scallions, cut into 2-inch sections, and finely shred into thin strips (there should be about ½ cup). Set aside on the same plate.

Cooking:
Heat a pan or wok over medium heat until very hot. Beat the eggs well. Add 1 tablespoon of the oil to the pan, then add the eggs. Slowly push the eggs back and forth until dry. Break into very small pieces and transfer to a plate. Reheat the pan and add the remaining 3 tablespoons oil. Add the shredded scallions and stir-fry for 30 seconds. Add the pork and stir-fry until it turns color and separates into strips. If the meat begins to stick to the pan, add a little more oil. Add the shredded cabbage, salt, and monosodium glutamate. Stir over high heat for 2 minutes. Add the cooked eggs and stir to heat through. Add the sesame oil and stir until well blended. Serve hot as a filling for 12 Mandarin Pancakes (page 172) or with Plain Rice (pages 153-155). The dish can be cooked ahead of time, omitting the eggs. Cook the eggs before serving, reheat the meat and vegetables, and combine.

Yield: 4 servings. Since the quantity of meat is small, this recipe may be doubled if you wish.

Choice of meat: After being trimmed, the meat may be partially frozen to facilitate slicing. Instead of pork cutlet, you may use hip or center pork chop or fresh ham, cut into strips; boneless, skinless chicken breast, cut with the grain into strips; or veal cutlet, flank, sirloin, or shell steak, cut with the grain into strips.

Choice of vegetable: Instead of cabbage, you may use 2 cups frozen French-style green beans, cut into 2-inch-long sections, and cook for 1 minute only.

Authentic Mu Shu Pork ingredients: Traditionally, ½ cup presoaked day lily buds and 2 cups presoaked tree ears are used instead of shredded cabbage.

Niu Jou Sung

CHOPPED BEEF WITH PEAS

½ pound lean ground beef (about 1 cup)

Marinade:
  2 teaspoons cornstarch
  1 tablespoon dry sherry
  ½ teaspoon sugar
  2 tablespoons soy sauce
  ⅛ teaspoon monosodium glutamate

  1 package (10 ounces) frozen peas (completely
      thawed)
  2 tablespoons peanut or corn oil
  ½ tablespoon cornstarch combined with
  2 tablespoons cold water

If an ingredient in the basic recipe is not readily available, see the list at the end of the recipe.

Preparation:
Combine the ground beef with the marinade ingredients. Mix well and set aside, along with the peas.

Cooking:
Heat a pan or wok over medium heat until very hot. Add the oil, then the beef. Stir-fry over medium heat until the meat separates and has mostly changed in color. Turn the heat to high and add the peas and mix them in with the meat, letting them cook together for 1 minute. Mix the cornstarch-and-water combination

well. Slowly add this to the meat and peas while you continue stirring until the sauce thickens and coats everything with a clear glaze. Serve hot with Plain Rice (pages 153-155).

Yield: 2 to 3 servings. Since the quantity of meat is small, this recipe may be doubled if you wish.

Choice of meat: Chopped veal, pork, boneless, skinless breast of chicken, or squabs may be used instead of beef.

Choice of vegetables: You may use frozen peas and carrots, diced parboiled green beans, zucchini, mushrooms, water chestnuts, or bamboo shoots.

Choice of exotic ingredients and another serving style: You may add 6 chopped freshly dried oysters (soft) or ½ can (3¼-ounce can) chopped smoked oysters and 1 tablespoon oyster sauce to the meat and peas before thickening with cornstarch and water. To use this as a first course, take 16 lettuce leaves (bibb, Boston, or iceberg), trim each leaf to form a cup approximately 4 inches in diameter, and fill with about 2 tablespoons of meat and peas. The guests are able to eat these with their fingers—6 servings as a first course.

Ch'ao Hsien Kan Pei

STIR-FRIED FRESH SCALLOPS

1 *pound fresh sea scallops*

Marinade:
1 *small egg white*
2 *teaspoons cornstarch*
½ *teaspoon salt*

2 *teaspoons minced fresh gingerroot*
1 *clove garlic, minced*
1 *teaspoon crushed red pepper*

Sauce:
1 *teaspoon sugar*
1 *teaspoon cornstarch*
1 *teaspoon distilled white vinegar*
1 *teaspoon sesame or corn oil*
2 *tablespoons soy sauce*
1 *tablespoon dry sherry*
1 *tablespoon cold water*

1 *cup peanut or corn oil*

If an ingredient in the basic recipe is not readily available, or if a variation is desired, see the list at the end of the recipe.

Preparation:
Rinse scallops several times in cold water. Drain and dry well with paper towels. Slice the scallops into

40

¼-inch pieces and set them in a bowl. Add the marinade ingredients to the scallops, using your hand to mix well. Place in the refrigerator for 30 minutes, or as long as 24 hours.

Prepare the gingerroot, garlic, and red pepper and set aside on a large plate in separate piles. Combine the sauce ingredients in a cup.

Cooking:
Place a strainer over a bowl near the cooking area. Heat a pan or wok over high heat until it is very hot. Add the oil and heat until moderately hot, about 300°. Add scallops to poach in the oil, and stir quickly to separate the pieces. When most of the scallops have changed color, pour them and the oil into the strainer to drain. As soon as the oil has drained away, set the scallops aside on a plate, saving the oil in the refrigerator for other cooking. The scallops can be prepared up to this stage an hour ahead of serving time.

Before serving, reheat the pan with 2 tablespoons of the drained oil. Add the gingerroot first and cook for 5 seconds. Then add the garlic and crushed pepper; stir and cook for 5 seconds. Add the partially cooked scallops, and stir-fry over high heat until very hot. Do not overcook. Mix the sauce ingredients very well and pour them into the pan, stirring until the sauce thickens and a clear glaze coats the scallops. Serve hot with Plain Rice (pages 153-155).

The stir-fried scallops may be added to the top of a stir-fried vegetable and served as a one-dish meal with Plain Rice.

Yield: 4 servings. This recipe may be doubled; poach the scallops in the oil 1 pound at a time, and then stir-fry the entire 2 pounds at once.

Choice of seafood and fish: Instead of sea scallops, you may use bay scallops—do not cut, leave whole; shrimp, shelled and deveined, and if large, split into halves; or fillet of gray sole, sea bass, yellow pike, or scrod, cut into 2 × 1-inch pieces.

Choice of seasonings: To give this dish a delicate flavor, you may omit the gingerroot, garlic, and crushed pepper, and use 1 teaspoon salt instead of the 2 tablespoons soy sauce in the sauce ingredients.

Choice of exotic ingredients: To give color and texture, you may add 1 cup soaked dried tree ears; stir-fry them together with the scallops.

Mien Pao Hsia Jen

DICED SHRIMP WITH CROUTONS

This is a famous northern dish from the Shantang province. The fried croutons will not soak up all the sauce from the dish; they will remain partially crispy.

1 *pound raw shrimp, shelled and deveined*

Marinade:
1 *small egg white*
2 *teaspoons cornstarch*
½ *teaspoon salt*

3 *slices firm white bread without crust*
½ *cucumber*
1 *cup peanut or corn oil*

Sauce:
2 *teaspoons cornstarch*
1 *teaspoon salt*
½ *teaspoon sugar*
⅛ *teaspoon ground white pepper*
1 *tablespoon dry sherry*
½ *cup chicken broth*

If an ingredient in the basic recipe is not readily available, or if a variation is desired, see the list at the end of the recipe.

Preparation:
Wash and dry, then dice the shrimp. Add the marinade ingredients and mix well. Refrigerate at least 30 minutes, or as long as 24 hours.

Dice the bread into ⅜-inch cubes (you should have 1½ cups). Cut the unpeeled cucumber lengthwise and remove the seeds. Dice into ⅜-inch cubes, to make about ¾ cup. Set aside with the croutons on a large plate. Combine the sauce ingredients in a small cup and set aside.

Cooking:
Heat the oil in a pan or wok to about 350° and fry the croutons until golden brown. Remove and spread on a clean brown paper bag to drain.

Place a strainer over a bowl near the cooking area. Heat the oil again to about 300°, add the shrimp, and quickly stir until the shrimp separate and the color changes. Then pour them and the oil into the strainer. As soon as the oil drains away, remove the shrimp to a dish. Refrigerate the cooled oil for future cooking use. The shrimp and croutons can be prepared up to this stage an hour ahead of serving time.

Before serving, reheat the pan. Add 2 tablespoons of the drained oil and stir-fry the cucumber. Mix the sauce well, then slowly pour it into the pan, stirring constantly until the sauce acquires a clear glaze. Add the cooked shrimp, combine with the sauce, and cook until the shrimp are just heated through. Add the croutons and stir once. Remove from the pan and serve immediately.

Yield: 4 servings. If more servings are desired, or for a more substantial meal, read the menu-planning chapter, page 6.

Choice of seafood: Diced bay or sea scallops may be used instead of shrimp. Frozen baby shrimp may be used (see Sizzling Rice dish, page 93, for instructions on how to use them).

Choice of vegetable: You may use ¾ cup diced zucchini, fresh peas, or frozen peas with carrots instead of cucumber.

Tan Chiao

PORK OMELETS WITH CELERY CABBAGE

½   pound ground pork
2   teaspoons cornstarch
1   tablespoon soy sauce
1   teaspoon salt
¼   teaspoon monosodium glutamate
1   tablespoon dry sherry
1   scallion, finely chopped
4   large eggs, beaten
1½ pounds celery cabbage
1½ cups chicken broth
4   tablespoons peanut or corn oil
1   teaspoon salt
½   teaspoon sugar

If an ingredient in the basic recipe is not readily available, or if an exotic variation is desired, see the list at the end of the recipe.

Preparation:
In a bowl, combine the pork, cornstarch, soy sauce, salt, monosodium glutamate, sherry, scallion, and eggs and mix them together very well. Set aside. Cut the celery cabbage into 2 × 1-inch strips and set aside along with the chicken broth.

Cooking:
Heat a large frying pan over medium heat until it is very hot. Add about 1 tablespoon of the oil to coat the bottom of the pan. Take a tablespoon of the egg-and-

meat mixture and place it in the pan to make a 2½-inch omelet. Make as many 2½-inch omelets as you have room for in the pan. While each omelet is still soft, fold it in half and cook until it is lightly browned. Then brown the other side in the same manner. Remove from the pan when cooked. Repeat this procedure, adding more oil as needed, until no more of the egg-and-meat mixture remains.

Reheat the pan, add the remaining oil, and stir-fry the celery cabbage until it starts to wilt. Add the chicken broth, salt, and sugar. Arrange the pork omelets on top of the cabbage. At this stage you may either leave the dish as it is and finish the cooking later or transfer the cabbage and omelets to a cook-and-serve casserole and prepare for serving.

Before serving, bring the liquid in the casserole to a boil, cover, and cook over medium heat for 15 minutes, or until the cabbage is soft and tender. This makes a fine one-dish meal with Plain Rice (pages 153-155).

Yield: 4 servings. The recipe may be doubled.

Choice of meat or seafood: Ground beef may be used instead of pork. Or half and half finely chopped shrimp and pork may be used.

Choice of vegetable: 2 ounces presoaked cellophane noodles, cut into 4-inch sections; 1 cup sliced bamboo shoots, combined with 2 cups mushrooms; 1½ pounds bok choy or spinach; or 2 bunches watercress may be used instead of celery cabbage.

Huo T'ui Tsai Hua

CAULIFLOWER WITH HAM

6 *dried Chinese black mushrooms (optional)*
1 *small head cauliflower*
3 *tablespoons peanut or corn oil*
½ *cup thinly sliced cooked Smithfield or country
   ham, each piece ⅛ × 1½ × 1 inch*
1 *teaspoon salt*
½ *teaspoon sugar*
2 *tablespoons water*
1 *teaspoon cornstarch combined with
   2 tablespoons water (optional)*

Preparation:
Wash and soak the mushrooms in warm water for 30 minutes. Cut off and discard the stems and cut each cap in half. Cut the cauliflower with stem into uniform-size flowerets with stem about 1½ inches long and ½ inch thick (you should have about 6 cups). Set aside on a plate with the ham.

In a saucepan, add 4 cups water and bring to a boil. Add the cauliflower and bring to a boil again, then immediately rinse in cold water and drain well. This can be done ahead of time.

Cooking:
Heat a wok or pan over moderate heat until it is very hot. Add the oil, then the cauliflower, mushrooms, and ham slices. Stir-fry for 1 minute. Add the salt, sugar,

and 2 tablespoons water. Mix well. Let cook over high heat for another minute. Serve hot.

1 teaspoon cornstarch combined with 2 tablespoons water may be added to this dish to thicken and coat the vegetables and meat at the last minute of cooking.

Yield: 4 servings.

Choice of vegetables: If you wish to substitute broccoli, use 6 cups and prepare it in the same manner as the cauliflower. Asparagus should be peeled, washed, and drained well, then cut diagonally into ½-inch pieces (you will need 6 cups). To use celery cabbage or bok choy, cut the stems into 2 × 1-inch pieces and the leaves into 2 × 2-inch pieces and increase the amount to 8 cups.

Ch'ao Lung Hsia

LOBSTER WITH MEAT SAUCE

1   1½-pound live lobster (ask the fish store to split
    the live lobster lengthwise and crack the big
    claws)
2   teaspoons minced fresh gingerroot (optional)
2   scallions, finely chopped
1   clove garlic, minced
¼   pound ground pork (½ cup)
3   tablespoons peanut or corn oil
1   tablespoon dry sherry
1   teaspoon salt
½   teaspoon sugar
¼   teaspoon ground white or black pepper
1   tablespoon soy sauce
½   cup chicken broth
½   tablespoon cornstarch combined with
    3 tablespoons water
2   large eggs

If an ingredient in the basic recipe is not readily available, or if an exotic variation is desired, see the list at
the end of the recipe.

Preparation:
Using kitchen shears, cut off all the lobster's feet and
claws. Save the feet from the top joints and discard the
bottom hairy ones. Cut the claws into small pieces,
each piece with the meat exposed. Remove the head
and cut in half. Discard the gills, sand bag, and large
part of the shell. Remove the vein in the back of the

body and cut each half of the body into 1-inch-long sections. Set all the pieces on a dish, including the juice and roe if any.

Set aside the gingerroot, scallions, and garlic on a plate with the ground pork.

Cooking:
Heat a pan or wok until very hot. Add the oil and stir-fry the gingerroot first, then add the garlic, ½ of the scallions (save the remaining ½ for the garnish), and pork together and stir until the pork separates. Add the cut-up lobster and stir-fry for 2 minutes. Sprinkle the sherry over the lobster. Add the salt, sugar, pepper, soy sauce, and broth. Mix well, cover, and bring to a boil. Let cook for 3 minutes over high heat.

Mix the cornstarch and water well. Slowly pour this into the sauce in the middle of the pan, stirring until the sauce boils and thickens. Beat the egg briefly. Slowly pour it into the pan. Remove the pan from the heat and dish out. Serve hot with Plain Rice (pages 153-155).

Yield: 2 servings.

Choice of seafood and seasonings: Instead of lobster, you may use 1 pound raw shrimp, shelled and deveined, split in half if large. Stir-fry with the chopped meat for 1 minute. Omit the 3 minutes of cooking over high heat; just add the seasonings, broth, cornstarch-water thickening agent, and egg. You may also add 2 teaspoons coarsely chopped salted black beans along with the pork; but reduce the salt to ½ teaspoon.

Ch'ao Sheng Ts'ai

STIR-FRIED ROMAINE LETTUCE

Leafy vegetables contain a large amount of water. The fresher and tenderer the plant, the more water released when cooked. Therefore, the amount of salt to be added to 1 pound of vegetables depends on their quality as well as on individual taste. Stir-fried leafy vegetables make a perfect accompaniment to the red-cooked or other meat dishes in the next chapter.

  1 *head romaine lettuce (about 1 pound)*
  3 *tablespoons peanut or corn oil*
  ¾ *teaspoon salt*
  1 *tablespoon soy sauce*
  1 *teaspoon sugar*

Other leafy vegetables may be used instead of romaine. See the list at the end of the recipe.

Preparation and cooking:
Wash the romaine lettuce and drain well. Cut the leaves into 2-inch sections. Heat a wok or a pot over high heat until very hot. Add the oil. Take as much lettuce as you can hold with both your hands and put it into the wok, in such a way that the vegetables cover the oil so it will not spatter. Add the remaining lettuce. Stir once or twice and add the seasonings. Continue to stir-fry just until the leaves of the romaine begin to wilt. Serve either hot or cold.

Yield: 4 servings.

Choice of vegetables: 1 pound of iceberg and Boston lettuce may be prepared in the same manner as romaine; cut Belgian endive into 1-inch sections; for spinach, amaranth, chrysanthemum greens, mung bean sprouts, or watercress (2 bunches), use 1 teaspoon salt, ½ teaspoon sugar, and omit the soy sauce; for asparagus, peel, wash, and drain well, then cut diagonally into thin slices, using 1 teaspoon salt, ½ teaspoon sugar and omitting the soy sauce (it only needs 1 to 2 minutes of stir-frying, then sprinkle with 1 to 2 teaspoons water, for it should retain a crispy texture). To make this dish fancier and tastier, add ½ cup sliced, sautéed fresh mushrooms to any of the above vegetables. You may use stir-fried spinach, watercress, amaranth, or chrysanthemum without the gravy and place the vegetables alongside the dish of Red-cooked Pork Shoulder (pages 64-65), Red-cooked Squabs (pages 70-71), or Braised Fresh Mushrooms (page 72) for a delicious one-dish-meal.

Ch'ao Ts'ai Hua

STIR-FRIED CAULIFLOWER

The vegetables used in the following two recipes contain relatively less liquid than the leafy vegetables. They may be served after being cooked just long enough to remove the raw taste or cooked until they are tender. If you wish to save time, they may be parboiled ahead of time and will only need a few minutes for stir-frying. Add the seasoning and a thickening agent consisting of 1 teaspoon cornstarch combined with 2 tablespoons water just before serving time.

- 1 *small head cauliflower (about 1 pound)*
- 3 *tablespoons peanut or corn oil*
- 1 *teaspoon salt*
- ½ *teaspoon sugar*
- 2 *tablespoons water*
- ⅛ *teaspoon ground white pepper*

Other vegetables may be used instead of cauliflower. See the list at the end of the recipe.

Preparation and cooking:
Cut the cauliflower into small flowerets with 1 inch of stem attached, approximately 2 × ½ × ½-inch in size. Wash and drain well. Heat a wok or pan over high heat until hot, add the oil, then add the cauliflower. Stir a few times and add the salt, sugar, and water. Cover and cook 1 to 2 minutes; add the ground pepper. Serve hot.

Yield: 4 servings.

Choice of vegetable: You may prepare 1 bunch broccoli in the same manner as cauliflower, but first peel the tough layer of the stems. Or cut 1 head cabbage into 1-inch squares, then separate the leaves. Or cut the stem of 1 head bok choy into 1-inch sections and the leaves into 2-inch sections. Or to use celery, peel off the outer layer of each stalk of 1 head, break stalks in half, pulling off any tough veins, and cut into 1-inch sections.

Choice of exotic flavors, texture, and color: Add 2 tablespoons chopped Szechuan preserved vegetable to give a tang to the dish. Or add 1 cut-up red sweet pepper or ¼ cup thinly sliced carrots, water chestnuts, or bamboo shoots, or 1 small can cream of corn to give it more color and texture. You may top the cooked vegetables with stir-fried meat, fish, or seafood for a one-dish meal. You may use 1 teaspoon cornstarch combined with 2 tablespoons water as a thickening agent. Mix well and add to the pan at the last minute of cooking.

Ch'ao Tou Chiao

STIR-FRIED GREEN BEANS

  1 *pound green beans*
  3 *tablespoons peanut or corn oil*
  ½ *teaspoon salt*
  ½ *teaspoon sugar*
  2 *tablespoons soy sauce*
  ⅓ *cup water*

Other vegetables may be used instead of green beans. See the list at the end of this recipe.

Preparation and cooking:
Snap off the ends of the green beans and break the beans into 2-inch sections. Wash and drain. Heat a wok or pan over moderate heat until hot and add the oil. Add the beans and stir-fry for 2 to 3 minutes. Add the seasonings and water, cover, and cook for 5 minutes for tender but crisp beans. Or cover and cook over medium-high heat for 30 minutes. The beans will be softer but will have a delicious, more concentrated flavor. Increase the sugar to 1½ teaspoons. Serve hot, or the softer beans may also be served cold.

Yield: 4 servings.

Choice of vegetable: You may use yard-long beans and prepare in the same manner as green beans; sweet green peppers (about 1½ pounds), with seeds and pith removed and cut into 1½ × 1-inch pieces; 3 medium cucumbers, peeled, with seeds removed, and cut into 1½ × ½-inch pieces (omit the water; cucumber has a large amount of water). To use eggplant (1 medium), remove and discard the stem, but do not remove the peel. Cut into 2 × 2 × ½-inch pieces. Increase the water to ½ cup. It may be cooked with 1 green pepper; adjust the seasoning. To use soybean sprouts (1 pound), remove and discard the roots. Soybean sprouts require a longer cooking time. Allow them to simmer 10 minutes before serving. To use 1 pound fresh mushrooms, slice if large and cut into halves if small. Stir-fry with oil for 15 minutes, add 1 tablespoon soy sauce, and omit the salt, sugar, and water.

Red-Cooked (Stewing) Casserole Dishes

NAME OF DISH	NATURE OF DISH	PAGE
Hung Men Ma Ku Braised Fresh Mushrooms	Excess moisture is removed from the mushrooms by stir-frying. Just enough soy sauce is added to give a more concentrated flavor.	72
Su Yü Braised Fish with Scallions	This sweet-and-sour-flavored fish can be kept in a covered container for weeks in the refrigerator. An excellent small dish for Plain Rice.	73

Red cooking refers to a stewing process in which meats, fish, or vegetables are slowly cooked with soy sauce; they actually appear more brown than red and can be cooked in large quantities. These dishes have a strong flavor and are usually seasoned with additional soy sauce. Red-cooked dishes are called "rice-sending dishes," because they are more salty and tend to have a concentrated gravy; hence, they are well complemented to rice and usually result in a higher level of rice consumption. Foods simmered with soy sauce can be kept in the refrigerator for long periods and are very good served cold. They can be reheated easily and, if done properly, will not lose their original texture. They are a very flavorful method of cooking.

Hung Shao Niu Jou

BRAISED SHIN OF BEEF

This dish has a concentrated flavor and should always be accompanied by mildly flavored dishes, such as salad dishes or stir-fried vegetables. It is also a good idea to put half of the dish away for another meal. If stored in the refrigerator, use within a week; if stored in the freezer, it may be kept up to a month.

2 pounds boneless shin of beef
2 tablespoons peanut or corn oil
2 scallions, cut into 2-inch-long sections
4 thin slices fresh gingerroot (optional)
2 teaspoons sugar
½ teaspoon salt
3 tablespoons soy sauce
2 tablespoons dry sherry
1 cup water
2 carrots, peeled and cut into 1-inch chunks

Preparation and cooking:
Cut the beef into 1-inch chunks. Heat a heavy pot until very hot. Add the oil and ½ of the beef chunks. Stir to seal well on all sides, then remove. Stir and seal the remaining beef chunks. Put the beef back into the pot and add the scallions, gingerroot, sugar, salt, soy sauce, sherry, and water. Mix well and bring to a boil. Cover and cook over medium-low heat for 30 minutes. Reduce the heat to low and let simmer for about 1½ hours, or until the meat is tender. Add the cut-up car-

rots on top of the beef without mixing in, cover, and turn the heat to medium-high for 15 minutes.

There should be about ¾ cup liquid left with the beef. If there is more liquid, uncover the pot, turn the heat up to high, and reduce the liquid to the desired amount. Serve the meat and carrots on a plate with the sauce. Serve hot with rice or steamed buns.

Yield: 6 servings.

Choice of meat: Instead of boneless shin of beef, use chuck, short rib, or other inexpensive cuts of beef. Cut into small pieces. For oxtail, disjoint and cook at least 2 hours longer. For pork butt or shoulder, cut into 1-inch chunks, cook for a total of about 1 hour, or until it is tender, and omit the carrots. For chicken legs and thighs, cut or leave whole, cook about 30 to 45 minutes, and omit the carrots. To prepare shin of beef in 1 piece, cook 1 hour longer. Let cool and keep in the refrigerator until it becomes firm, then thinly slice and serve as an appetizer with or without the sauce. The sauce can be heated or jellied.

Choice of seasonings: Cook 1 to 2 whole star anises with the meat and remove before serving. Or add 2 to 3 dried whole red peppers and cook with the meat; remove before serving.

Kan Shao Niu Jou Pien

SPICY BEEF

This is a typical Szechuan dish, peppery hot and without gravy. It can be served hot or cold in a small portion for an appetizer, or as a small side dish, spicy beef will add zest to a dinner if one finds the meal too bland. To properly use it as a main dish, serve it with a stir-fried fresh vegetable and Plain Rice (pages 153-155). This dish will keep well in a covered container in the refrigerator for as long as 2 weeks.

2   pounds fillet of chuck (top chuck)
2   teaspoons crushed red chili pepper
½   teaspoon Szechuan peppercorns (optional)
2   cloves garlic, crushed
6   thin slices fresh gingerroot
¼   cup corn oil
2   tablespoons dry sherry
1   teaspoon salt
1   tablespoon sugar
¼   cup soy sauce

If an ingredient in the basic recipe is not readily available, see the list at the end of the recipe.

Preparation and cooking:
Slice the steak into 2 × 1 × ⅛-inch pieces. Set aside on a plate with the chili pepper, peppercorns, garlic, and gingerroot.

Heat a saucepan until hot. Add the oil, then the chili pepper and gingerroot. Fry until the pepper turns slightly brown. Add the garlic, peppercorns, and beef. Stir until all the beef changes color. Sprinkle with sherry, then add the salt, sugar, and soy sauce. Cover and, stirring occasionally, cook over medium-high heat for about 20 minutes, or until the sauce is almost gone. The chili pepper, peppercorns, gingerroot, and garlic may be removed before serving.

Yield: 4 servings as a main dish.

Choice of meat: Sirloin or fresh, lean ham may be used instead of top chuck.

Hung Shao T'i Tzu

RED-COOKED PORK SHOULDER

1   5-pound *fresh pork picnic shoulder, with the skin
    and bone*
2   *scallions, cut into 2-inch-long sections*
3   *tablespoons rock or light brown sugar*
½   *cup soy sauce*
½   *cup dry sherry*

Preparation and cooking:
Place the pork shoulder skin-side up in a large pot and
add enough water to cover. Bring the water to a boil
and allow to boil for 10 minutes. Discard the cooking
water and rinse the meat under warm water. Put the
meat back in the pot skin-side up.

Place a heat-taming pad over the burner and set the pot
over it. Turn the heat to high. Add the scallions, sugar,
soy sauce, sherry, and enough water to almost cover
the pork shoulder. Cover the pot and bring to a boil.
Turn the heat to medium and cook for 30 minutes, then
to medium-low and simmer for about 4 to 5 hours, or
until the meat and skin are soft enough to be picked off
with chopsticks or a fork.

Skim off and discard the fat from the gravy, and cook,
uncovered, over higher heat until the gravy reduces to
about 1 cup. During this time, baste the gravy over the
skin several times. Transfer the meat to a deep platter
and pour the sauce over it. The meat may be separated

from the bone, sliced with the skin on, and served with the gravy. This is a good dish to serve with plain boiled rice or steamed buns. The dish can be cooked ahead of time and reheated.

Leftover red-cooked pork is good cold: Remove the bones, cut into thin slices, and garnish with jellied gravy. Or heat the jellied gravy and pour over the cold meat.

Yield: 8 to 10 servings.

Choice of meat: Pigs' knuckles can be cooked the same way. Reduce the cooking time to 2 to 3 hours.

Choice of exotic ingredients: Add 8 presoaked Chinese black mushrooms or 1 cup soaked day lily buds or 6 hard-cooked eggs 30 minutes before skimming the fat.

Shih Tzu Tou

LION'S HEAD

2 tablespoons cornstarch
2 tablespoons cold water
1 pound ground boneless pork butt with some fat (about 2 cups)
½ cup meat or chicken stock
3 tablespoons soy sauce
1 large egg
1 pound celery cabbage
1 tablespoon peanut or corn oil
½ teaspoon sugar

If an ingredient in the basic recipe is not readily available, or if an exotic variation is desired, see the list at the end of the recipe.

Preparation:
In a large mixing bowl combine 1 tablespoon of the cornstarch and 1 tablespoon of the cold water. In another dish combine the remaining cornstarch and water and set aside. Add the ground pork to the mixing bowl, stir with a spoon, and gradually mix in ¼ cup of the stock. Add 2 tablespoons of the soy sauce and the egg. Stir some more, in one direction only, until the meat holds together. Set aside.

Rinse and drain the cabbage. Cut the stalks lengthwise into ½-inch pieces, then crosswise into 3-inch-long sections (there should be about 6 cups). On the bottom of a 2- to 3-quart heatproof casserole or Dutch oven arrange about ¼ of the cut-up cabbage in 1 layer. Set aside.

66

Cooking:
Heat a large skillet. Add the oil to coat the pan. Divide the meat mixture into 4 portions, pat each portion into a round ball, and coat each ball with the remaining cornstarch-and-water mixture. Put the meatballs into the skillet and fry until slightly brown. Gently remove the meatballs and place them on the bed of cabbage strips in the casserole. Browning the meatballs is optional; they may also be placed on the bed of cabbage strips immediately after being coated.

Reheat the skillet and stir-fry the remaining cabbage for 2 minutes. Add the sugar, the remaining 1 tablespoon soy sauce, and the remaining stock. Place the stir-fried cabbage on top of the meatballs in the casserole, cover tightly, and slowly bring to a boil. Let simmer for 2 hours. This dish may be prepared in advance. When reheating it, use low heat to bring it slowly to a simmer.

Yield: 4 servings.

Choice of meat and other variations: If you wish to use veal or beef, add 2 tablespoons oil to the meat mixture in addition to the other ingredients.

For a more elaborate dish: Peel and finely chop 4 large fresh water chestnuts and add them to the meat. Or add ½ cup finely chopped ham to the meat. Or add 1 cup cooked crab meat to the meat, along with 1 teaspoon salt and 1 teaspoon minced fresh gingerroot. Bok choy or cabbage may be used instead of celery cabbage.

Chiang Yu Chi

SOY SAUCE CHICKEN

This is a simple way to cook soy sauce chicken. It is a substantial dish which can be cooked ahead of time and served warm or cold for all occasions. For best results, use a freshly killed chicken. The soy sauce will coat the chicken more evenly and give it a better color.

1 *roasting chicken (about 4 pounds)*
2 *teaspoons salt*
¼ *cup soy sauce*
¼ *cup dry sherry*
1 *tablespoon sugar*
2 *whole star anises (optional)*
¾ *cup water*
1 *teaspoon sesame or corn oil*

If an ingredient in the basic recipe is not readily available, see the list at the end of the recipe.

Preparation and cooking:
Clean and dry the chicken as well as the gizzard and heart. Sprinkle the inside of the chicken with salt. To make it easier to turn the chicken while cooking, tie a string around the base of its neck.

Put the rest of the ingredients, except the sesame oil, in a large pan, preferably a wok with a heat-taming pad, and bring to a boil. Stir to dissolve the sugar. Add the chicken and cook, covered, at a slow boil over medium-low heat. Turn the chicken every 10 minutes. To avoid breaking the skin, insert a wooden spoon into the chicken cavity. Holding on to the string, lift it before turning. Cook for about 40 to 50 minutes. The last turn should leave the chicken breast-side down. Remove from the heat and allow it to stand for 5 minutes with the cover on.

Place the chicken on a plate and brush it with additional sesame oil. Then place it in the refrigerator to cool for about 30 minutes, or until the juice is slightly congealed. There should be about ½ cup of rich gravy.

Serve the Soy Sauce Chicken in the same manner as you would roast chicken. Or serve it cut up Chinese style: Cut the cooled chicken through both the skin and the bones into 1 × 2-inch pieces and pour either hot or room-temperature gravy over it. Do not reheat the chicken.

Yield: 8 servings. If more servings are desired, or for a more elaborate meal, read the menu planning chapter, page 6.

Choice of fowl: Cornish hen, duck, or squab may be cooked the same way. Two pounds of blanched chicken livers or gizzards may be cooked the same way, 20 minutes for livers and 30 minutes for gizzards. Omit the salt, add 2 tablespoons of oil, and the sauce will be absorbed.

Hung Shao Ke Tzu

RED-COOKED SQUABS

> 2 *fresh squabs*
> ¼ *cup soy sauce*
> 1 *teaspoon sesame or corn oil*
> 1 *scallion, cut into 2-inch sections*
> 2 *slices crushed fresh gingerroot*
> 2 *teaspoons sugar*
> ¼ *cup water (approximately)*

Preparation:
Clean the squabs. Put them in a container and add the soy sauce and sesame oil. Cover and marinate the squabs for 2 to 3 days in the refrigerator, turning them several times.

Cooking:
Place the squabs breast-side down in a heavy pot along with the marinade. Add the scallion, gingerroot, and sugar, then add the water, cover, and bring to a boil. Cook over low heat for 1½ hours, turning the squabs every 30 minutes. When cooked, the squabs are chopstick-tender, with very little gravy remaining. Skim off the fat. If there is too much gravy, turn the heat higher and cook a little longer to reduce the liquid. Serve hot.

Yield: 2 servings. This recipe can be multiplied successfully.

Choice of other poultry: Fresh rock cornish hens or a small duckling may be used instead of squabs.

Choice of additional vegetables in the dish: Stir-fry 1 pound of spinach or 2 bunches watercress without gravy and serve as a garnish around the dish to make this an elegant one-dish meal with Plain Rice (pages 153-155).

Hung Men Ma Ku

BRAISED FRESH MUSHROOMS

There are two ways of cooking fresh mushrooms. One way is to stir-fry them in oil for 2 minutes and season with soy sauce or salt. The other way is to stir-fry in oil for 15 to 20 minutes, so that the mushrooms' moisture will evaporate, then season them with soy sauce or salt. They are wonderful served hot or cold, combined with plain stir-fried vegetables, or chopped up and used as a filling in dumplings.

1 *pound fresh mushrooms*
4 *tablespoons corn oil*
1 *tablespoon soy sauce or ¾ teaspoon salt*

Preparation:
Quickly wash and drain the mushrooms. If the mushrooms are small, cut into halves, and if they are big, cut them into slices through the stem into the cap.

Cooking:
Heat a pan or wok until very hot. Add the oil and stir-fry the mushrooms over medium heat for 15 to 20 minutes, or until the mushrooms' liquid has evaporated. Add soy sauce and mix well. Serve either hot or cold. The mushrooms can be cooked ahead of time, then quickly reheated and served hot.

Yield: 1½ cups. 4 servings.

Su Yü

BRAISED FISH WITH SCALLIONS

1½ pounds *whole butterfish (about 6 small ones)*
12 *small scallions, cut into 4-inch-long sections*
1 *teaspoon salt*
¼ *cup sugar*
¼ *cup soy sauce*
¼ *cup distilled white vinegar*
2 *tablespoons corn oil*
2 *tablespoons sesame or corn oil*

Preparation:
Clean and wash the fish. Set the scallions aside along with the fish. Put ⅓ of the cut-up scallions in the bottom of a heavy saucepan, then layer ⅓ of the fish on top of it. Continue alternating layers of fish and scallions. Sprinkle on top the salt, sugar, soy sauce, vinegar, and the corn and sesame oils. Place the saucepan on the burner and bring to a boil, cover, and cook over low heat for about 2 hours. Do not move the fish but baste them with the sauce once or twice. There should be some sauce left when the dish is done. The small bones become so soft that you can eat all parts except the spine. Serve cold.

The fish taste better if cooked a day ahead, and this dish will keep up to 2 weeks in a covered container in the refrigerator.

Yield: 4 to 6 servings. This recipe can be multiplied successfully.

Choice of fish: Small smelts or other fine-textured small fish may be used instead of butterfish.

73

Deep-Fried, Poached, and Oven-Cooked Dishes

NAME OF DISH	NATURE OF DISH	PAGE
Hsia Ho Shrimp Puffs	Excellent with drinks and as an appetizer.	90
Kuo Pa Puffed Rice	A basic recipe; used for a snack and an interesting addition to several dishes.	91
Hsia Jen Kuo Pa Seafood and Meat Sizzling Rice	Shrimp, meat, and other ingredients in a rich gravy are poured over hot puffed rice to make a sizzling noise—a dramatic dish and a good one-dish meal for company.	93
Kuo Pa T'ang Sizzling Rice Soup	Another dramatic dish popular all over China and abroad.	96
Pai Shui Hsia Poached Shrimp with Shells	An easy-to-prepare dish that is also excellent as an appetizer.	97
K'ao Chi Kuan Broiled Chicken with Ginger Sauce	Well-seasoned chicken pieces that can be served hot or cold—good for picnics.	98
Ch'a Shao Chinese Roast Pork	Marinated pork strips, roasted in the oven. They can be eaten hot or cold, cooked with vegetables, or added to fried rice or noodles.	100

Deep frying is a method of cooking that tends to scare people because they immediately think of greasy food. However, if the food is cooked properly, many times it is not any more greasy than food that has been stir-fried. In Chinese cooking, frying in oil is done at different temperatures, according to the particular food, and this results in different textures. For example, when frying batter-coated foods and egg rolls, the oil should be hot before the food is put in. By contrast, shrimp balls should be fried in oil at a lower temperature and for less time to avoid crust formation and minimize shrinkage.

T'ien Suan Chi T'iao

SWEET-AND-SOUR CHICKEN

2 small whole boneless, skinless chicken breasts (about ¾ pound)

Marinade:
- ½ tablespoon soy sauce
- ½ teaspoon sugar
- 1 teaspoon salt
- ¼ teaspoon white pepper
- 1 teaspoon cornstarch

2 tablespoons peanut or corn oil

Sweet-and-Sour Sauce:
- 1 clove garlic, thinly sliced
- 1 green pepper, cored, seeded, and cut into 1-inch cubes
- ½ small carrot, sliced
- ½ cup canned pineapple chunks with some pineapple juice
- ¼ cup distilled white vinegar
- ¼ cup sugar
- 1 tablespoon soy sauce
- ½ cup chicken broth

Batter:
- ¾ cup all-purpose flour
- ¼ cup cornstarch
- 2 teaspoons baking powder

½ teaspoon salt
¾ cup cold water (approximately)

2 cups peanut or corn oil
1 tablespoon cornstarch combined with
   3 tablespoons water

If an ingredient in the basic recipe is not readily available, or if an exotic variation is desired, see the list at the end of the recipe.

Preparation:
Cut the chicken into 1½-inch-long and ½-inch-wide strips. Combine the marinade ingredients, add the chicken, and set aside.

Heat the 2 tablespoons oil in a saucepan. Add the garlic, green pepper, and carrot; stir-fry for 2 minutes. Remove the cooked vegetables from the pan. Add the pineapple, vinegar, sugar, soy sauce, and chicken broth to the same saucepan. Stir to dissolve the sugar and set the pan aside, to be heated later.

Combine all the batter ingredients, using a wire whisk to mix them into a smooth and thin batter, and adding more water if it seems too thick.

Cooking:
Heat a wok or deep-frying pan. Add the 2 cups oil and heat to about 375°. While the oil is being heated, take about 2 tablespoons warm oil from the wok and add to the batter. Mix well. Mix the marinated chicken again

and add it to the batter. Using chopsticks or a spoon, drop a few at a time of the coated chicken pieces into the hot oil and fry for 3 minutes on both sides. The chicken pieces should be crisp and brown. Fry the rest of the batter-dipped chicken. Keep warm in the oven with the door ajar.

Bring the sauce to a boil, stirring constantly. Add the cornstarch-and-water mixture and stir until the sauce clears and thickens. Add the cooked vegetables. Mix to blend. Serve either poured over the fried chicken or in a sauceboat as a dip.

The fried chicken can be reheated by frying for 1 to 2 minutes in 375° oil or by placing for 5 minutes in a preheated 450° oven.

Yield: 4 servings. If more servings are desired, or for a more substantial and elaborate meal, read the menu planning chapter, page 6.

Choice of meat, fish, or seafood: If you wish to use pork tenderloin or boneless pork butt, cut the pork into 1-inch cubes and blanch in boiling water for 2 minutes. To use fillet of sole, sea bass, yellow pike, or scrod, cut the fish into the same size pieces as the chicken (1½ × ½ inches). To use shrimp, remove all shells except the tail sections of the shrimp. Split the back sides and remove the veins. For fish and seafood, omit the soy sauce and sugar in the marinade.

Choice of vegetable: Sliced celery, snow pea pods, water chestnuts, or bamboo shoots and mushrooms may be used instead of green pepper.

Choice of exotic dips: To make Roasted Salt and Szechuan Peppercorns, combine 2 tablespoons coarse salt with 1 teaspoon Szechuan peppercorns; heat in a dry pan for about 5 minutes, or until slightly brown, then crush finely with a mortar and pestle. To make Vinegar and Tabasco Dip, combine ¼ cup wine vinegar with ½ to 1 teaspoon Tabasco sauce.

Choice of sauce: Lemon Sauce may be used instead of Sweet-and-Sour Sauce. The recipe follows:

2 *large lemons, thinly sliced*
2 *tablespoons peanut or corn oil*
1 *cup chicken broth*
1 *teaspoon salt*
3 *tablespoons sugar*
1 *tablespoon cornstarch*

Stir-fry the lemon slices in the oil for 30 seconds. Combine the remaining ingredients very well, making sure that the cornstarch and sugar are dissolved. Add this sauce to the stir-fried lemon and stir until it thickens and forms a clear glaze. This sauce may be used on any of the above-mentioned deep-fried foods.

Ho T'ao Chi Kuan

DEEP-FRIED WALNUT CHICKEN

2 small *whole boneless, skinless chicken breasts* (about ¾ *pound)*

Marinade:
1 egg *white*
3 tablespoons *cornstarch*
1½ teaspoons *salt*
1 tablespoon *dry sherry*
⅛ teaspoon *white pepper*

2 *cups peanut or corn oil*
1½ *cups walnuts, finely chopped*
Salt and pepper to taste

Preparation and Cooking:
Cut chicken into 1½ × 1 × ¼-inch pieces. Combine chicken with the marinade ingredients. Using your hand, mix well. Keep in refrigerator for 30 minutes.

Heat the oil to about 375°. Take the chicken pieces out of the marinade 1 at a time and coat with the chopped walnuts. Deep fry in hot oil until golden. Drain and serve hot. They may be sprinkled with salt and pepper before serving.

Yield: 8 servings as an appetizer. 3 to 4 servings as a main dish.

Choice of nuts: If walnuts are not readily available, peanuts, cashews, or almonds may be used.

Cha Ch'ieh Tzu

DEEP-FRIED EGGPLANT

Batter:
 ¾ cup all-purpose flour
 ¼ cup cornstarch
 2 teaspoons baking powder
 ¾ cup cold water (approximately)

 1 medium eggplant (about 1 pound)
 2 cups peanut or corn oil
    Salt to taste

If an ingredient in the basic recipe is not readily available, or if an exotic variation is desired, see the list at the end of the recipe.

Preparation and cooking:
Combine all the batter ingredients and, using a wire whisk, mix the batter until smooth. The batter should be like thick cream; add more water if it is too thick.

Wash the eggplant, remove and discard the stem, but do not peel. Cut the eggplant crosswise into ¼-inch slices. Cut again into 2 × 2-inch pieces. Heat the oil to about 375°, but while it's heating, add 2 tablespoons of the warm oil to the batter and mix in. Coat the eggplant pieces with the batter and deep fry in the hot oil until the outside is lightly browned and crispy and the inside is soft. Drain and sprinkle with salt and serve hot. The eggplant can be fried ahead of time and reheated on a rack in a 425° oven for 5 minutes, or until crispy. The fried eggplant is good served with Plain Rice (pages 153-155).

Yield: 8 to 10 servings as an appetizer. 4 servings as a main dish.

Choice of vegetable: Instead of eggplant, you may deep fry 1 pound of the following vegetables in the same manner: sliced fresh mushrooms or zucchini; the tender leaves and stems of chrysanthemum greens; scallions, cut into 2-inch lengths; Chinese white turnips or carrots, grated; whole bean sprouts. All can be dipped in batter and fried.

Choice of exotic dips: To make Hoisin Sauce Dip combine ¼ cup hoisin sauce, 2 tablespoons water, 2 teaspoons sugar, and 1 teaspoon sesame oil, and mix well. To make Roasted Salt and Szechuan Peppercorns, combine 2 tablespoons coarse salt with 1 teaspoon Szechuan peppercorns in a dry frying pan. Heat for about 5 minutes, or until slightly brown, then crush finely with a mortar and pestle.

Hsia Jung

SHRIMP PASTE

  1 *pound fresh raw shrimp, shelled and deveined*
  ¼ *cup ground fresh pork fat or blanched fatty bacon*
  2 *egg whites*
  1 *tablespoon cornstarch*
1½ *teaspoons salt*
  ⅛ *teaspoon white pepper*
  1 *tablespoon dry sherry*

If an ingredient in the basic recipe is not readily available, or if an exotic variation is desired, see the list at the end of the recipe.

Preparation:
If a food processor is used, blend the shrimp and pork fat until very fine. Add the remaining ingredients and blend until the mixture forms a smooth paste.

If a meat grinder is used, beat the egg whites until foamy. Using the fine plate, grind the shrimp and pork fat twice, then mix into a smooth paste. Combine with the remaining ingredients and egg whites.

If a cleaver is used, make the paste in the same manner as with a meat grinder, except that the cleaver is used to chop the shrimp into a fine paste.

The shrimp paste can be prepared up to 24 hours in advance and kept in a covered container in the refrigerator.

This shrimp paste is used for Fried Shrimp Balls (page 85), Poached Shrimp Balls (page 86), Stir-fried Shrimp Balls with Vegetables (page 88), Shrimp Ball Soup (page 87), and Shrimp Puffs (page 90).

Choice of ingredients: Frozen small shrimp may be used instead of fresh shrimp (see the recipe for Seafood and Meat Sizzling Rice, page 93, for instructions on how to use them). Add ¼ teaspoon monosodium glutamate to the shrimp in addition to the other ingredients. Add about 4 large fresh or canned water chestnuts to the shrimp in addition to the other ingredients to give additional texture.

Cha Hsia Chiu

FRIED SHRIMP BALLS

2 *cups peanut or corn oil*
1 *recipe Shrimp Paste (page 83)*

Preparation and cooking:
Have ready a small bowl of cold water, a tablespoon, a strainer, and a plate lined with paper towels.

Heat a wok until very hot. Add the oil and heat over medium heat to about 325°. With your left hand, take a handful of the shrimp paste and squeeze your fingers into a fist, forcing the paste up between your thumb and forefinger and forming a ball about the size of a walnut. With your right hand, use a tablespoon dipped in the cold water (to prevent sticking) to scoop up the shrimp ball and drop it into the hot oil. Turn the balls so that they fry evenly. Fry for about 2 minutes, or until the balls float to the top and become fluffy. Do not overcook; overfrying will shrink the shrimp balls. Scoop up the shrimp balls with a strainer and hold them over the wok to drain. Place the cooked shrimp balls on the paper towels, then transfer to a serving platter. Serve hot with salt and pepper. The shrimp balls can be frozen and reheated in a preheated 350° oven for 7 to 8 minutes.

Yield: 24 shrimp balls, each 1 inch in diameter. 4 servings as a main dish. Serve with a stir-fried vegetable or salad and Plain Rice (pages 153-155).

Choice of dip: See Sweet-and-Sour Chicken (page 76).

Chu Hsia Wan

POACHED SHRIMP BALLS

This recipe is a precooked poaching method for making two shrimp ball dishes: Shrimp Ball Soup and Stir-fried Shrimp Balls with Vegetables, the recipes for which follow.

1 recipe Shr'mp Paste (page 83)

Preparation ar d cooking:
Make shrimp balls, using the same technique described on page 00. But instead of dropping the shrimp balls into oil, drop them into a pot containing 4 cups cold water. Place over medium heat. When the water just begins to boil, gently stir once, turn the heat to low, and let simmer for 1 minute. Drain and put into a pot of cold water. Drain again.

Storing:
Prepare a container with enough cold water to cover the shrimp balls. Keep the shrimp balls in the cold water until ready to use. They can be stored in a covered container in the refrigerator for up to 3 or 4 days. They are now ready to be used in the recipes for Shrimp Ball Soup (page 87) and Stir-fried Shrimp Balls with Vegetables (page 88).

Yield: 24 shrimp bal's, each 1 inch in diameter.

Hsia Wan T'ang

SHRIMP BALL SOUP

    4 cups chicken broth
    1 recipe Poached Shrimp Balls (page 86)
    2 teaspoons finely chopped scallion
    1 teaspoon salt
    ⅛ teaspoon white pepper
    ½ teaspoon soy sauce

Cooking:
Pour the chicken broth into a saucepan. Add the drained Shrimp Balls to the broth. Slowly bring to a boil. Turn the heat to low and simmer for 5 minutes. Add the chopped scallion and the remaining ingredients. Serve hot.

Yield: 8 servings as a first course. 4 servings as a main course.

Choice of exotic ingredients: Add 2 ounces of presoaked cellophane noodles and a small bunch of tender watercress cut into 1-inch sections. Adjust the seasoning. This is an excellent one-dish meal when served with Plain Rice (pages 153-155). You may also add 1 to 2 teaspoons fish sauce instead of soy sauce.

Ch'ao Hsia Wan

STIR-FRIED SHRIMP BALLS WITH VEGETABLES

1   cup sliced fresh mushrooms
2   cups sliced peeled cucumber
1   scallion, cut into 2-inch-long sections
3   tablespoons peanut or corn oil
1   recipe Poached Shrimp Balls (page 86)
1½ teaspoons salt
¼   teaspoon sugar
⅛   teaspoon white pepper
¾   cup chicken broth
1½ teaspoons cornstarch combined with
      2 tablespoons water

Preparation:
Prepare the sliced mushrooms, cucumber, and scallion
and set on a large plate along with the drained Poached
Shrimp Balls.

Cooking:
Heat a pan or wok over medium heat until hot. Add the
oil and stir-fry the mushrooms and cucumber for 2
minutes. Add the scallion and Shrimp Balls, stir, and
mix. Add the salt, sugar, pepper, and chicken broth.
Cover and cook over medium-high heat for about 3 to 5
minutes. Stir the cornstarch and water well and slowly
pour into the pan, stirring until all ingredients are
coated with a light, clear glaze. Serve hot with rice.

Yield: 4 servings. If more servings are desired, or for a more substantial and elaborate meal, read the menu planning chapter, page 6.

Choice of vegetables: 1 cup presoaked black dried Chinese mushrooms, straw mushrooms, bamboo shoots, or water chestnuts, and 2 cups of snow pea pods, cut-up broccoli, or asparagus may be used instead of fresh mushrooms and cucumber.

Hsia Ho

SHRIMP PUFFS

20 *very thin slices of white bread*
 1 *recipe Shrimp Paste (page 83)*
 2 *cups peanut or corn oil*

Preparation and cooking:
Using a 1½-inch diameter round cookie cutter, cut each slice of bread into 4 crustless disks. Use a sandwich spreader to spread about 1 heaping tablespoon Shrimp Paste on each bread disk, topping with another bread disk. Deep fry the shrimp puffs, a few at a time, in 325° to 350° oil for 2 minutes on each side. Remove and drain on paper towels. Keep warm in the oven while you fry the rest. The cooled or leftover shrimp puffs can be frozen and reheated in a 400° oven for about 5 minutes.

Yield: 40 shrimp puffs, great for an appetizer. 4 servings as a main dish.

Kuo Pa

PUFFED RICE

Puffed Rice is a most delicious and inexpensive snack. It is also used in two other dishes: Seafood and Meat Sizzling Rice (page 93) and Sizzling Rice Soup (page 96). Both make satisfying one-dish meals and are impressive dishes to serve guests because of the sizzling sound they make at the dining table. The cooking can be simplified by advance preparation.

1½   cups long-grain rice
 2   cups cold water
 3   cups peanut or corn oil

Preparation:
Wash and drain the rice several times. Put the rice and cold water in a 10 × 15-inch jelly-roll pan and spread the rice evenly to make a thin layer. (If a smaller pan is used, adjust the quantities of rice and water accordingly.) Let stand for 30 minutes.

Cooking:
Cover the pan with aluminum foil and bake in a preheated 375° oven for 30 minutes. Remove the foil, wet the back of a spatula, and lightly press the rice down. Reduce the heat to 325° and continue baking the rice, uncovered, for about 1 hour. The rice should be dry at the sides of the pan, but the center will still be damp.

Let the rice dry at room temperature for 24 hours, or until the rice patties are thoroughly dry. Break the dried rice patties into approximately 2 × 2-inch pieces. These dried rice patties can be kept for a long time and fried when needed.

Fry the dried rice patties in very hot oil (about 400°), 2 pieces at a time for about 5 seconds on each side. Drain. The rice patties will puff up, double in size, and will be light brown and crispy. For snacks or appetizers, sprinkle on fine salt while the Puffed Rice is still warm. Do not salt when they are to be used in other dishes, such as Seafood and Meat Sizzling Rice or Sizzling Rice Soup. The Puffed Rice can be kept crisp in a tightly covered container for weeks.

Choice of rice: Oval grain or glutinous rice may be cooked in the same way, using ½ cup less water.

Hsia Jen Kuo Pa

SEAFOOD AND MEAT SIZZLING RICE

1 pound frozen baby shrimp, shelled and deveined
2 teaspoons salt

Marinade for shrimp:
½ egg white
2 teaspoons cornstarch
½ teaspoon salt
¼ teaspoon monosodium glutamate

2 ½-inch-thick boneless pork chops, thinly sliced

Marinade for pork:
1 teaspoon cornstarch
1 tablespoon water
1 tablespoon soy sauce
1 tablespoon dry sherry

1 cup sliced fresh mushrooms or ½ cup sliced canned mushrooms
1½ cups thinly sliced zucchini

Sauce:
1 cup chicken broth
½ teaspoon salt
⅛ teaspoon white pepper
1 tablespoon cornstarch
1 tablespoon soy sauce

6 tablespoons peanut or corn oil
6 Puffed Rice patties (see page 91)

Preparation:
Thaw the shrimp. Let them soak in 2 cups cold water combined with the 2 teaspoons salt for 30 minutes. Drain and dry well. Combine the shrimp with the shrimp marinade ingredients; mix well and keep in the refrigerator for at least 30 minutes, or as long as 24 hours. Combine the pork slices with the pork marinade ingredients; mix well. Prepare the mushrooms and zucchini and set aside on a plate. Combine the sauce ingredients in a bowl.

Cooking:
Heat a wok or pan over medium heat until it is very hot. Add 4 tablespoons of the oil and stir-fry the shrimp until they become firm and most of their color changes. Remove with a slotted spoon and set aside on a plate. Using the same pan and the leftover oil, stir-fry the pork in the same manner; if it is too dry, add some oil. Remove and set aside along with the cooked shrimp.

Before serving:
Preheat the oven to 450°. Put the Puffed Rice on a heatproof serving platter and heat in the oven for 7 to 8 minutes. Meanwhile heat a wok or pan over medium heat with the remaining 2 tablespoons oil. Stir-fry the mushrooms and zucchini for 2 minutes. Stir the sauce ingredients, making sure the cornstarch is well mixed. Slowly pour the sauce into the pan, stirring until it forms a light, clear glaze. Turn the heat to high, then add the cooked shrimp and meat, stirring quickly until they are just heated through. Remove and transfer to a hot serving dish.

Take both the serving platter with the hot Puffed Rice and the hot serving dish to the dinner table. Pour the cooked shrimp and vegetables over the Puffed Rice to make a sizzling noise in front of the diners. Serve immediately.

Yield: 6 servings.

Choice of meat and seafood: 4 ounces of veal, beef, or chicken may be used instead of pork. 1 pound of scallops, lobster, or crab meat may be used instead of shrimp. Fresh shrimp may be used instead of frozen, in which case omit the saltwater soaking process.

Choice of vegetables: Broccoli and asparagus may be used instead of mushrooms and zucchini. Presoaked Chinese dried black mushrooms or canned straw mushrooms, water chestnuts, bamboo shoots, snow pea pods, or baby corn may also be used as substitutes.

Choice of broth: Instead of homemade broth, canned chicken broth without vegetable flavorings may be used.

Kuo Pa T'ang

SIZZLING RICE SOUP

To make Sizzling Rice Soup, you prepare the meat, seafood, and vegetables as for Seafood and Meat Sizzling Rice (page 95). Just adjust the sauce ingredients as outlined below to make a clear soup base. When serving, add the hot Puffed Rice to the hot soup in front of the diners.

> 1 recipe Seafood and Meat Sizzling Rice (page 93), minus the sauce ingredients

Sauce:
> 4 cups chicken broth (if canned broth is used, dilute with half water)
> 1 teaspoon salt, or to taste
> ¼ teaspoon white pepper, or to taste

Yield: 6 servings.

Pai Shui Hsia

POACHED SHRIMP WITH SHELLS

1 pound medium raw shrimp with shells (about 28
to 30 shrimp), preferably fresh
1 chunk fresh gingerroot, crushed
1 scallion, cut in half
2 tablespoons dry sherry

Sauce:
2 tablespoons light or regular soy sauce
1 teaspoon sugar
1 tablespoon sesame or corn oil
1 teaspoon hot red pepper oil or ¼ teaspoon ground
red pepper, more or less to your taste

Preparation:
Use a scissors to cut off the shrimp feet. Open a small
section of each back and pull out the vein. Wash the
shrimp and drain well.

In a saucepan, bring 1 quart water to a boil. Add the
gingerroot and scallion and let boil for 2 minutes. Add
the cleaned shrimp and bring to a boil again. Splash on
the sherry, then immediately cover the pan. Turn off
the heat, leave the pot covered, and let the shrimp sit in
the hot water for 1 minute. Drain and serve hot with the
sauce as a dip.

Yield: 4 servings as main dish. 6 servings as an appetizer.

K'ao Chi Kuan

BROILED CHICKEN WITH GINGER SAUCE

This chicken dish has a Chinese flavor, but it can be served in Western style, using forks and knives. The cooked chicken can also be cut into small chunks and eaten with chopsticks. It goes well with Plain Rice (pages 153-155).

12 chicken thighs or 6 legs (about 2 pounds), or a whole chicken (about 3 pounds)
 1 teaspoon salt
 2 scallions, finely chopped
 1 clove garlic, minced
 2 tablespoons minced fresh gingerroot
 2 tablespoons peanut or corn oil
 ¼ cup soy sauce
 1 tablespoon sugar
 1 tablespoon sesame or corn oil

Preparation:
If chicken legs are used, cut each leg into 2 pieces; if a whole chicken is used, cut into 12 pieces. Sprinkle the salt over the chicken pieces and set aside.

Prepare the scallions, gingerroot, and garlic and set aside in separate piles on a plate.

Heat a pan or wok. Add the oil and lightly brown the ginger, then add the scallions and garlic and stir-fry for 1 minute. Add the soy sauce and sugar and bring to a boil. Turn off the heat and add the sesame oil. Put the cut-up chicken in the sauce and marinate for at least 1 hour before cooking.

Cooking:
Place the chicken pieces meat-side up in a pan on the lower rack of the broiler and broil at 450° for about 25 minutes, or until golden brown. Baste once with the leftover marinade. Turn the chicken pieces over and broil for 20 minutes more. Do not baste again in order that the skin may become crispy. Serve hot.

Yield: 4 servings.

Ch'a Shao

CHINESE ROAST PORK

2 pounds boneless pork butt

Marinade:
 2 teaspoons salt
 1½ tablespoons sugar
 ¼ teaspoon white pepper
 2 teaspoons honey
 3 tablespoons soy sauce
 2 tablespoons dry sherry
 1 tablespoon peanut or corn oil

If an ingredient in the basic recipe is not readily available, or if an exotic variation is desired, see the list at the end of the recipe.

Preparation and cooking:
Cut the pork into strips about 6 to 8 inches long, 2 inches wide, and ½ inch thick. If the thickness is uneven, split the thick part and flatten with the back of a cleaver.

Combine the marinade ingredients. Add the pork strips. Let them marinate at room temperature for at least 2 hours, turning several times, or as long as 24 hours in the refrigerator.

Preheat oven to 425° and roast the pork strips on a rack over a pan of water for about 40 minutes. Turn over once. You will see that they are slightly burned around the edges. Slice and serve hot. The roast pork keeps well in the refrigerator for 3 to 4 days or in the freezer for several weeks.

Yield: 6 servings.

Choice of uses: This recipe may be doubled. Keep the unused portion in the freezer. Completely thaw the pork when needed and reheat in a 400° oven for 5 to 10 minutes. Cut-up roast pork may be combined with any fresh or frozen vegetables to make a perfect one-dish meal with Plain Rice (pages 153-155). Diced roast pork may be used with fried rice and shredded pork goes well with noodles.

Choice of meats: Loin or shoulder pork chops, country ribs, or shoulder pork may be cooked in the same way. Trimmed spareribs may be used but roast as a whole piece and cut into ribs just before serving. Veal or lamb ribs may be used instead of pork.

Choice of seasonings: One tablespoon hoisin sauce may be added to the marinade to give it a slightly sweet and pungent taste, and you may add 2 cloves fresh garlic or ¼ teaspoon garlic powder as well.

Steamed Dishes, Soups, and Firepots

NAME OF DISH	NATURE OF DISH	PAGE
Kan Kao T'ang Chicken Liver Custard Soup	An elaborate puréed soup. It requires a blender or a food processor to get the right consistency.	121
Tan Hua T'ang Egg Drop Soup	A basic recipe that can lead to many other exotic and delicate soups.	123
Chi Yi T'ang Chicken Wings with Gingerroot Soup	This delicious meaty soup is made with simple ingredients and goes well with Plain Rice.	125
Niu Jou T'ang Beef and Vegetable Soup	Another hearty soup for a family meal.	127
Hua Kuo Firepot	A firepot, good for a one-dish meal and fun entertainment for guests in cold weather. There are variations for Chrysanthemum Firepot, Mongolian Firepot, and Ten Varieties Firepot.	129

Steaming is one of the key Chinese cooking methods and is just as important as oven cooking. However, in contrast to the Western method of cooking in a double boiler, that is, cooking over the steam, the Chinese method of steaming is cooking in the steam, using moist heat. Different, too, from baking in an oven with dry heat or frying, steaming has the added advantages that it does not require cooking oil, creates no objectionable odors, and requires minimal cleanup. Finally, steaming lets you conserve fuel, since you can cook more with a given amount of heat simply by adding layers to the steamer.

A typical Chinese steamer is composed of a base full of water (either a large fitted pot or a wok), on top of which is placed one or more tiers of perforated racks with rims 2 to 4 inches high, and finally a cover. The base is usually aluminum, but the racks and cover can be bamboo, metal, or a combination. The bamboo steamer is the most desirable because it transfers heat more evenly and absorbs extra moisture. On the other hand, metal tiers are somewhat more practical, as they are easier to clean, are lighter in weight, and will not burn should the pot boil dry.

However, steaming foods does not necessarily require special implements. For example, if the food to be steamed is in a deep dish, such as a soup, one can simply place it on a metal rack in the bottom of a large pot or one can improvise by using an inverted heat-resistant bowl instead of a rack. In either case, be sure there is free-flowing water between the bottom of the pot and the food dish, and that the rim of the food container is 2 inches above the water level. Additionally, use a food dish that is narrower than the pot, to allow steam to circulate freely. Generally, about 2 inches of water should be used in order to avoid boiling dry. If a shallow platter is used, as you might when steaming a whole fish, a higher rack should be used to avoid having the water boil over and into the food. For steaming larger amounts (for example, a batch of buns), a Chinese steamer should probably be used on top of the fitted base of a wok about 2 inches wider than the steamer racks.

Cheng Jou Ping

STEAMED GROUND PORK

This steamed ground pork dish is similar to the American meat loaf. It is easy to cook, subtle in flavor, and good with Plain Rice (pages 153-155) for family meals. There are many variations of this dish.

¾ pound ground pork (about 1½ cups)
1 teaspoon salt
1 tablespoon soy sauce
1 tablespoon dry sherry
1 tablespoon finely chopped scallion
2 large eggs, beaten

Preparation:
In a mixing bowl combine the ground pork, salt, soy sauce, sherry, and scallion. Stir the mixture in one direction only, until the meat holds together. Add the eggs, mix, and blend well with the meat.

Transfer the meat mixture to a soup plate or an 8-inch pie plate. Smooth the surface evenly. The meat is now ready to be cooked. It can be kept in the refrigerator for several hours and removed 30 minutes before cooking.

Cooking:
Set up a steamer and bring the water to a boil over medium-high heat. Put the meat plate in the steamer, cover, and steam for 20 minutes. Turn off the heat and let stand for 5 minutes. Lift the hot dish from the steamer and set on a plate. Serve hot.

Yield: 4 servings.

Choice of meat: Chopped veal or beef may be used instead of pork. Add 1 tablespoon peanut or corn oil along with other ingredients while mixing.

Choice of exotic ingredients: Slice 2 Chinese sausages crosswise into ¼-inch pieces and arrange on top of the meat mixture before steaming. In the basic steamed ground pork recipe, omit the salt, and use 2 salted duck eggs and 1 fresh egg. Separate the whites from the yolks of the salted duck eggs. Mix the salted egg whites and the fresh egg with the meat mixture, then transfer to a pie plate. Smooth the meat mixture down evenly. Make 4 dents in the meat for the duck egg yolks. Cut each yolk in half and put a half in each space, round-side up. Steam according to the directions. You may also add 1 section preserved salty fish, about 3 × 4 inches, either canned or dried. The Chinese have many different kinds of preserved fish. Most of them are salty but very tasty. The Ningponese are well known for their preference for salty fish. I can predict that you will eat more rice when you have this dish, but remember to take only a very small portion of the fish to begin with. Wash and clean the fish well. Presoak in cold water for 30 minutes if the fish is dried. Cut into ½-inch strips. Lay on top of the meat-and-egg mixture and steam according to directions. You may also add 2 tablespoons chopped *cha ts'ai* (Szechuan preserved vegetable). Mix with the meat and reduce the salt to ½ teaspoon.

Huo T'ui Cheng Chi

STEAMED CHICKEN WITH HAM

2 *whole chicken breasts (about 2 pounds)*
6 *very thin slices fresh gingerroot, each piece*
   1 × 2 × ⅛ inch

Marinade:
1 *teaspoon salt*
2 *teaspoons cornstarch*
1 *tablespoon soy sauce*
1 *tablespoon peanut or corn oil*

2 *large ⅛-inch-thick slices cooked Smithfield ham*
   (about ¼ pound)

Preparation:
Remove the chicken breastbone but leave the skin on.
Cut the poultry through the skin and into 1-inch pieces.
Put the chicken pieces in a mixing bowl. Add the
gingerroot and the marinade ingredients. Mix and toss
to coat the chicken pieces evenly. Arrange the chicken
on a large plate with a rim or on a 9-inch pie plate,
making 2 layers at the most. Cut the ham into 1 × 2-
inch pieces and set the ham pieces in between the
chicken pieces. The dish is now ready to be cooked. It
can be refrigerated, covered, for a few hours, but take
it out 30 minutes before cooking.

Cooking:
Set the plate in a preheated steamer, cover, and steam
over high heat for 20 minutes. Serve hot on the same

plate on top of a large platter. The gingerroot may be removed before serving. This dish is excellent served hot with rice.

Yield: 6 servings.

Choice of meat and other ingredients: Presoak about 6 large dried Chinese mushrooms until soft. Remove the stems and cut into halves. Add to the chicken along with the ham or use 2 Chinese sausages cut diagonally into 5 or 6 pieces in place of ham. And any other kind of ham may be used instead of Smithfield ham.

Chien Chi

SALTED CHICKEN

Salting a chicken before cooking not only gives a better flavor but also tenderizes the chicken. It is an easy way to prepare and cook a chicken. It can be prepared in advance and will keep well in the refrigerator. Because it is well seasoned, it can be served on any occasion, either as an appetizer or as a main dish with Plain Rice (pages 153-155) and a stir-fried vegetable. The salted cooked chicken can also be smoked.

1 *4-pound roasting chicken*
4 *tablespoons coarse salt, or use 1 tablespoon of coarse salt for each pound of chicken*

If an ingredient in the basic recipe is not readily available, or if an exotic variation is desired, see the list at the end of the recipe.

Preparation:
Wash the chicken, drain, and dry well. Sprinkle the salt both inside and outside the chicken. With your hand, rub in the salt thoroughly and evenly. It is important that the salt cover the entire chicken. Place the chicken in a container with a cover and store in the refrigerator for at least 2 days, or up to 4 days. Turn the chicken twice during this time.

Cooking:
Rinse the salted chicken, drain, and dry well. Set the chicken breast down in a large, deep dish. Use a pot or

steamer with a cover and fill with water at least 1½ inches deep. If using a pot, place a rack in the water (with a steamer there is no need to use a rack). Set the dish with the chicken on the rack. Cover tightly, bring the water to a boil, and steam for 45 minutes, or until the chicken meat starts to separate from the bone on the drumstick. About 1 cup of liquid will accumulate in the bowl during the steaming. Let the chicken cool for 15 minutes, then place it in the refrigerator to be slightly jellied. Save the chicken liquid for soup stock or gravy.

Cut the chicken into small pieces with the bone and skin or carve the chicken on your dining table. Eat the skin, for it will have a delightful texture; lick the bones, for they are simply delicious. Serve cold. It is easier to cut and will taste better.

Yield: 6 servings.

Choice of meat: Turkey parts such as the breast and the thigh or fresh or frozen duck may be used instead of chicken.

Choice of exotic ingredients: Before salting the chicken, use 2 chunks of crushed fresh gingerroot, 2 stalks crushed scallions, and 1 tablespoon dry sherry. Rub them inside and outside the chicken or duck with your hand. Discard the scallions and gingerroot. Then rub in 1 tablespoon Szechuan peppercorns along with the salt, as described in the recipe.

Choice of method of cooking: The salted chicken may be roasted like a regular roasting chicken. When roasting a salted duck—a 5-pound duck is the best choice—place the duck breast-side up directly on the oven rack. Place a broiler pan with 1 to 2 inches of water, about 4 inches below the duck. Roast for 45 minutes. Then turn it breast-side down and roast for another 45 minutes, or until the skin color is golden and crispy. Allow the duck to cool for 10 to 15 minutes, then cut it into small pieces and serve with the traditional lotus leaf buns, or use sliced white bread without crusts and steamed briefly in the steamer, as wrappers to sandwich the duck meat and skin.

Fen Cheng Pai Ku

STEAMED SPARERIBS WITH CREAM OF RICE

1 *scallion*

Marinade:
⅛ *teaspoon ground white pepper*
⅛ *teaspoon ground red pepper*
½ *teaspoon salt*
1 *teaspoon sugar*
2 *tablespoons soy sauce*
1 *tablespoon dry sherry*
2 *tablespoons water*

1½ *pounds spareribs (ask the butcher to chop the spareribs across the bones into 1¼-inch-long sections) or 1 pound pork butt, cut into 1 × 1½ × ½-inch pieces*
½ *cup cream of rice*

If an ingredient in the basic recipe is not readily available, or if an exotic variation is desired, see the list at the end of the recipe.

Preparation:
Trim and wash the scallion, cut it into 1½-inch-long sections, and shred these finely. Put the scallion in a large mixing bowl and add the marinade ingredients. Stir well to dissolve the salt and sugar. Set aside.

Cut the spareribs between each rib, but do not trim the fat (you will have about 3 cups). Wash and drain. Add the spareribs to the bowl with the marinade. Let stand for 20 minutes. Turn and mix several times while marinating.

Toast the cream of rice in a dry frying pan for 5 minutes, or until it is slightly brown. Let cool. Then coat each sparerib with the toasted cream of rice. Arrange the spareribs with the scallion shreds on a large soup plate or a 9-inch pie plate, making 2 layers at the most. Pour the extra marinade on top. The dish is now ready to be cooked. It can be kept in the refrigerator, covered, for a few hours, but take it out 30 minutes before cooking.

Cooking:
Place the plate of ribs in a steamer over medium-high heat for 1½ hours, or until the pork is tender. Have a kettle of boiling water ready on the stove to add to the steamer when it needs more water.

Check after 1 hour of steaming; if some cream of rice coating the ribs is still dry, turn the meat over and continue steaming for another 30 minutes. Serve hot. The dish can be cooked ahead of time and reheated by steaming.

Yield: 4 servings.

Choice of meat: To make Steamed Beef with Cream of Rice, use ¾ pound sliced boneless shell or flank steak instead of pork. Add ¼ teaspoon baking soda, 2 tablespoons water, ¼ cup peanut or corn oil, ¼ teaspoon ground red pepper, and ⅛ teaspoon monosodium gluta-

113

mate to the marinade in addition to the other ingredients. Preferably, steam directly in a bamboo steamer lined with vegetable leaves such as bok choy, lettuce, or cabbage. Steam for 20 minutes only.

Choice of exotic ingredients: Use ⅛ teaspoon ground Szechuan peppercorns instead of ground white pepper.

Cheng Yü

STEAMED FISH

¾ pound *fillet of scrod*
1 *teaspoon salt*
½ *teaspoon sugar*
1 *tablespoon dry sherry*
1 *tablespoon soy sauce*
2 *tablespoons peanut or corn oil*
1 *tablespoon finely shredded fresh gingerroot*
1 *scallion, split and cut into 2-inch sections*

If an ingredient in the basic recipe is not readily available, or if an exotic variation is desired, see the list at the end of the recipe.

Preparation:
Rinse the fish, dry with a paper towel, and sprinkle the salt evenly over the fillet. Place the fish on a plate with a rim. Add the sugar, sherry, soy sauce, oil, gingerroot, and scallion on top of the fish.

Cooking:
In a steamer bring the water to a boil. Place the dish containing the fish on a steaming rack. Cover tightly and steam over high heat for about 10 minutes. Remove the plate with the fish and place on top of a larger platter to serve. Serve hot.

Yield: 3 to 4 servings. If more servings are desired, or for a more substantial and elaborate meal, read the menu planning chapter, page 6.

Choice of other fish: Fillet of gray sole, shad, sea bass, red snapper, or whiting may be used instead of fillet of scrod. Best of all is a fresh whole fish, 1 to 1½ pounds, with the head and tail intact, such as sea bass, yellow pike, red snapper, whiting, gray sole, or butterfish. You may use 2 fish in the same dish. Always lay them in 1 layer side-by-side, never stacked on top of each other. If a large fish is used, slash the fish meat crosswise in 2 to 3 cuts on both sides. Steaming time depends on the thickness of the fish, for example, 1½ pounds of sea bass should be steamed for about 15 minutes, butterfish for 8 minutes. To test whether the fish is cooked or not, push a pair of chopsticks into the thickest part of the fish, making sure the sticks are not pushing against spinal bones. If the flesh is soft and there is no resistance to the prodding, the fish is done. Otherwise, continue steaming for 2 to 3 minutes and then test again.

Choice of exotic ingredients and cooking method: The 2 tablespoons oil, the gingerroot, and the scallion may be left out when the fish is steaming. Instead heat 3 tablespoons oil in a frying pan and brown the shredded gingerroot slightly. As soon as the fish is cooked, add the scallion on top of the fish and pour the hot oil over it to give a more concentrated flavor. You may add 2 teaspoons coarsely chopped fermented salted black beans to the fish in addition to the basic ingredients. Add about ¼ teaspoon ground red pepper with the black beans to give a spicy flavor.

Cheng Tan

STEAMED CLAM AND EGG CUSTARD

1 dozen *small clams*
4 *eggs*
½ *teaspoon salt*
2 *teaspoons peanut or corn oil*
2 *cups chicken broth*

If an ingredient in the basic recipe is not readily available, or if a variation is desired, see the list at the end of the recipe.

Preparation and cooking:
Soak the clams in cold water for at least 1 hour; scrub them clean and set aside.

Beat the eggs until the whites and yolks are well combined. Add the salt and oil to the eggs. Gradually beat the chicken broth into the egg mixture. Pour into a heatproof bowl with a 2- to 3-inch rim. Add the whole, unshelled clams.

Place the bowl on a rack in a pot or wok containing water up to 1 inch from the rim of the bowl. Cover and slowly bring to a boil. Let cook on low heat for about 30 minutes, or until the custard is smooth and a knife inserted in the center comes out clean. Serve hot.

Yield: 2 servings as a one-dish meal with Plain Rice (pages 153-155). 6 servings as a first course.

Choice of other ingredients: Shelled clams may be used instead of whole ones. Ask the fish dealer to open the clams. Reserve their juice and add it to the chicken broth, first removing an equal portion of the chicken broth so that the end result is just 2 cups. Also, ½ cup chopped pork, beef, or shrimp may be used instead of clams. Add 1 tablespoon soy sauce and 1 tablespoon chopped scallion to the meat before mixing with the eggs and other ingredients.

Chi T'ang

HOMEMADE CHICKEN BROTH

Obviously, this is not a one-dish meal but Homemade Chicken Broth is an important ingredient that will certainly improve any dish's flavor, particularly soups and gravies, when it is substituted for water. Chicken, duck, turkey or other poultry, or pork, particularly the more economical cuts (e.g. chicken backs, necks, and pork bones), can be used to make a rich broth.

Beef and lamb bones are not suitable in making broth for Chinese soups and gravies because they have very strong flavors. For Chinese broths, use only poultry, pork, or ham and small amounts of scallion; no other vegetables should be added.

    1 5-pound *fowl or* 5 *pounds of chicken backs and*
       necks
    3 *quarts water*
    1 *scallion*

Place the chicken or bones into a large pot along with the scallion and water. Bring to a boil, then turn heat down to a simmer. Remove the scum as much as possible. Partially cover and simmer for about 3 hours.

Let cool, then slowly and gently pour the broth out through a strainer, discarding the solids (or use the meat for other cooking). Skim most of the fat off the top of broth, but leave some to give the broth flavor. The broth can be stored in a covered container in the refrigerator for up to a week or in the freezer for up to 3 months.

For an extra clear broth, precook the poultry and bones as follows: Place the chicken meat and bones into a large pot of boiling water and boil for 2 to 3 minutes. Rinse the scum and fat off of the meat and bones; wash the pot, and proceed as above.

Yield: About 10 cups chicken broth. Use when a recipe calls for chicken broth, either as is or diluted to taste.

Choice of other broths: For convenience canned chicken broth can be used instead of homemade broths. However, be sure to choose a pure chicken broth with no vegetable additives. For soups, dilute 2 cups canned chicken broth with 1 cup water. For gravies, do not dilute. When a light, delicate flavor is desired, water with a pinch of monosodium glutamate can be used as in vegetarian cooking.

Kan Kao T'ang

CHICKEN LIVER CUSTARD SOUP

¼ pound chicken livers (about 3 pairs)
1 single boneless, skinless chicken breast (about 5 to 6 ounces)
2 large eggs
⅔ cup chicken broth
1 teaspoon salt, to taste
1 tablespoon dry sherry
¼ teaspoon ground white pepper
2 cups clear chicken broth
1 teaspoon minced scallion

If an ingredient in the basic recipe is not readily available, or if an exotic variation is desired, see the list at the end of the recipe.

Preparation and cooking:
Remove and discard as much as possible of the membrane and veins from the chicken livers and tendons from the chicken breast, then cut them into small pieces.

Combine the chicken breast, chicken livers, eggs, and the ⅔ cup broth in a food processor or blender and blend for 1 minute, or until it is very smooth. Add the salt, sherry, and pepper, and blend some more. Pour the mixture into 6 cups or bowls, filling each one only half full.

Set the cups in a pot or skillet filled with hot water to 1½ inches below the cups' rims. Cover and let simmer (not boil) for 20 minutes, or until the custard is just set.

Meanwhile, have ready the 2 cups clear chicken broth, brought to a boil, and seasoned with salt to taste. The custard may be steamed in a large soup bowl and simmered for 30 minutes, or until the custard is set. When the custard is done, use a small knife to loosen the sides and bottom, then add enough hot broth to fill the cup. Sprinkle the scallion over the top. Serve piping hot.

Yield: 6 servings as a first course. This is a rich soup. It makes 4 servings as a main dish and should be served with Plain Rice (pages 153-155) accompanied with a salad or a pickled vegetable.

Choice of meat: Instead of chicken livers, duck or calf liver may be used. And the liver may be cooked alone without the chicken meat. Increase the livers to 6 pairs.

Choice of exotic ingredients: Instead of scallion as a garnish, to each bowl add 2 pieces very thin, 2 × 1-inch slices of cooked Smithfield ham and fresh coriander leaves.

Tan Hua T'ang

EGG DROP SOUP

This basic recipe for egg drop soup can lead to many other exotic and delicate soups. Two important points: First, the right consistency and thickness of the corn-starch mixture must be attained, and second, it is essential that the egg be only barely cooked.

> 3 cups homemade pure chicken broth or
> 1 13¾-ounce can of pure chicken broth with
> enough water added to make 3 cups
> 1 teaspoon salt
> ⅛ teaspoon white pepper
> 1½ tablespoons cornstarch combined with
> ¼ cup water
> 2 large eggs
> 2 teaspoons sesame or corn oil

Cooking:
In a saucepan bring the broth to a boil. Add the salt and pepper. Mix the cornstarch and water together thoroughly and slowly add the mixture to the pan, stir-ring until the soup thickens and boils again. In a bowl, beat the eggs thoroughly. Remove the soup from the heat and slowly pour the eggs into the soup. Stir once. Pour the soup into a tureen or into individual bowls and garnish with the sesame oil. Serve at once.

Yield: 4 servings.

Choice of vegetables: Add 1 cup grated zucchini to the clear soup when you add the salt and pepper, adjusting

123

the saltiness to your taste; then add the cornstarch-and-water mixture and the eggs. Or add 1 10-ounce package frozen chopped spinach, thoroughly thawed, to the clear soup when you add the salt and pepper, adjusting the saltiness to your taste; then add the cornstarch mixture, but use only 2 egg whites instead of 2 whole eggs (beat the whites until stiff; remove the pot from the heat and slowly add the egg whites while stirring). If you add 1 8-ounce can cream of corn to the clear soup, bring everything to a boil and season with salt and pepper; omit the cornstarch-and-water mixture; beat 2 egg whites until stiff; remove the pot from the heat and slowly add the egg whites while stirring; omit the oil and sprinkle 1 tablespoon minced ham on top.

Chi Yi T'ang

CHICKEN WINGS WITH GINGERROOT SOUP

- 8 medium chicken wings (about 1½ pounds)
- 3 or 4 ½-inch-thick pieces fresh gingerroot, peeled and crushed
- 2 scallions, left whole
- 1 tablespoon peanut or corn oil
- ¼ cup dry sherry
- 5 cups boiling water
- 2 teaspoons salt, or to taste

If an ingredient in the basic recipe is not readily available, or if an exotic variation is desired, see the list at the end of the recipe.

Preparation and cooking:
Cut the wings apart at the joint. Remove and discard the tips and the extra skin at each joint of each chicken wing. Set aside with the gingerroot and scallions.

Heat a saucepan, add oil and the gingerroot, and stir-fry for 1 minute. Add the chicken wings, stirring constantly until the chicken pieces start to brown. Add sherry, stir, and quickly cover; cook for a few seconds. Add the boiling water, scallions, and salt; allow to return to a boil. Lower the heat and let simmer, covered, for about 30 minutes, or until the chicken wings are tender.

Remove scallions, skim off the fat, and serve hot. The gingerroot will not have lost too much of its zest from having been cooked and may be served with the chicken wings and soup.

Yield: 6 servings.

Choice of other fowl: Cut-up chicken legs or other parts of chicken may be used. Duck or squab may be used instead of chicken.

Choice of exotic ingredients: Wash and presoak until soft; 8 medium dried Chinese black mushrooms; add these along with the scallions. Wash and presoak until soft ½ cup dried flat-tip bamboo shoots; add these with the scallions along with their soaking water, but omit the salt. You may garnish with 10 2 × 1-inch thin slices cooked Smithfield ham before serving.

Niu Jou T'ang

BEEF AND VEGETABLE SOUP

2 pounds beef neck bones with meat attached (ask the butcher to chop each neck bone into 4 to 5 pieces, about 2 inches each)
2 tablespoons peanut or corn oil
1 medium yellow onion, peeled and quartered
4 cups combination of carrots, celery, and cabbage, cut into small pieces
4 cups boiling water
Salt, black pepper, and monosodium glutamate to taste

If an ingredient in the basic recipe is not readily available, see the list at the end of the recipe.

Preparation and cooking:
In a large saucepan, parboil the neck bones for 5 minutes. Discard the water and rinse the neck bones.

Heat the same saucepan. Add the oil and stir-fry the onion quarters until they are translucent. Add the carrots, stir and cook together for 2 minutes, then add the celery and cabbage and stir-fry together some more. Put the neck bones back in the pan, add the boiling water, cover, and allow it to return to a boil. Turn the heat down to low and let it simmer for 2 to 3 hours, or until the meat is soft and can be picked off with chopsticks. Remove and discard the bones, or you may eat directly from the bones. Season the soup with salt and pepper to taste and a pinch of monosodium glutamate.

Yield: 4 servings with Plain Rice (pages 153-155) or bread. Or add ½ pound dried (uncooked) rice sticks (rice noodles) or ½ pound cooked noodles or very thin spaghetti to the hot, cooked soup, bring to a boil, and cook for 1 minute. Pour into 4 individual bowls and serve as a lunch or light supper.

Choice of meat: Oxtail, shin, chuck, or pork neck bone may be used instead of beef neck bone.

Choice of vegetables: Green beans, beets, cucumber, collard greens, tomatoes, and soybean sprouts may be cooked with pork neck bones instead of onion and the the other vegetables listed.

Hua Kuo

FIREPOT

1 whole chicken cutlet, cut into 1 × 2 × ⅛-inch slices
1 pound tender beef, cut into 1 × 2 × ⅛-inch slices
½ pound raw shrimp, shelled, deveined, and split in half laterally
½ pound fillet of gray sole or yellow pike, sliced into 1 × 2 × ¼-inch pieces
1 dozen shelled clams or oysters
¼ pound calf or chicken livers, sliced into 1 × 2 × ⅛-inch pieces
1 teaspoon salt
¼ teaspoon white pepper
1 tablespoon dry sherry
1 tablespoon peanut or corn oil
2 ounces cellophane noodles, boiled in water for 5 minutes, left soaking until cool, and cut into 4-inch-long pieces
½ pound fresh spinach or romaine lettuce, washed and drained
2 pieces fresh tender bean curd, sliced into 2 × 1 × ½-inch pieces

Sauce:
2 eggs
½ teaspoon sugar
3 tablespoons light or dark soy sauce
2 tablespoons dry sherry
2 tablespoons sesame or corn oil

8 cups chicken broth

129

Preparation:
On 6 plates arrange the chicken, beef, shrimp, sole, clams, and liver in 1 layer, with pieces partially overlapping. Sprinkle the salt, pepper, sherry, and oil on top. Cover with clear plastic wrap and refrigerate until ready to serve.

Put the drained cellophane noodles, the spinach, and the bean curd in 2 serving bowls.

To prepare the sauce, beat the eggs thoroughly, then add the remaining ingredients.

Pour the chicken broth into either a traditional firepot or an electric casserole or skillet placed on the dining table. Bring the broth to a boil. The broth must continue to simmer during the time the dish is served and eaten.

Place 2 to 3 tablespoons of the prepared sauce in each of 6 individual rice bowls. Put the meat, fish, and vegetable plates and bowls on the table and allow each person to serve himself, holding chopsticks in one hand and the sauce bowl in the other.

Cooking at the dining table:
The proper method of cooking is for each person to use the chopsticks to dip a thin slice of meat, fish, or vegetable into the boiling broth and let it cook to the desired degree of doneness. The food is then dipped into the individual's sauce bowl and eaten while hot. You may serve steamed or baked rolls with the meal. The sauce should be used a little at a time as you eat.

Yield: 6 servings.

Choice of firepots: For Mongolian Firepot, instead of other meat, fish, and seafood, use 3 pounds lean leg of lamb only. For easy slicing, have the butcher remove the lamb bone, tendons, and gristle. Tie the meat with strings as for a roast. Freeze it until it is firm enough to cut with an electric slicer. Remove the strings and cut the meat into paper-thin slices. One-half pound of lamb is a good-size portion for each serving. Arrange in 1 layer, with pieces partly overlapping, on each of 6 plates. The other ingredients are the same. Use the peanut butter dressing in Noodle Salad (page 160). Dilute the dressing with ½ cup cold water. Place 2 to 3 tablespoons of the mixed sauce in each of 6 individual rice bowls.

For Ten Varieties Firepot, use 20 Fried or Poached Shrimp Balls (page 85 and page 86), ½ pound sliced Chinese roast pork (page 100) or cooked ham, ½ pound sliced shin of beef in one piece (listed in choice of meat section for Braised Shin of Beef, page 60), ½ recipe Pork Omelets with Celery Cabbage (use just the omelets, page 46), 1 dozen small clams, 2 ounces pre-soaked cellophane noodles, ½ pound blanched celery cabbage, and ½ cup each bamboo shoots and soaked dried mushrooms. Place a layer of cabbage and drained cellophane noodles in the firepot, then arrange in an attractive pattern the bamboo shoots, mushrooms, meat, and place the seafood on top. If the pot is not large enough, add more as the portions are eaten. Pour the chicken broth in along the side of the pot trying not to disturb the pattern of the food. Cover and bring to a boil and cook for 10 minutes. The food should be served piping hot, as soon as the clams have opened. Each guest should help him or herself from the pot. The difference with this pot is that guests do not have to cook, the food is precooked and seasoned. A dish of soy sauce should be served as a dip.

Salad Dishes

In Chinese cooking, salads may be made of raw, salted, blanched, or cooked ingredients mixed with a dressing. Typical ingredients in a Chinese salad are ham, egg, mung bean sprouts, cucumbers, celery cabbage (Chinese cabbage), lettuce, and so on, and with a dressing made from a mixture of vinegar, soy sauce, salt, sugar, and sesame seed oil.

Most of the vegetables in a Chinese salad are either salted slightly or parboiled beforehand, for various reasons. For example, many vegetables have a high water content; if one salts these vegetables ahead of time, some of these liquids will be drawn out, allowing one to prepare the salad without worrying about diluting the dressing. Thus, the seasoning can be better controlled. Also, salad vegetables are often parboiled so that they will not have an undesirable "raw taste," like a raw potato. Examples of such vegetables are celery cabbage and bean sprouts. Someone who cooks authentic Chinese dishes will never serve mung bean sprouts that have not been at least blanched, because the "raw taste" is very unpleasant to the Chinese palate.

Szechuan P'ao Ts'ai

SZECHUAN PICKLED CABBAGE

Szechuan pickled cabbage is a delicious homemade relish, and it can be made all year round. It can be served as a side dish or cooked together with meats or fresh vegetables. If you keep it in an aged brine for a long time, it will develop a very tasty sauerkrautlike flavor. A choice of exotic vegetables and seasonings that can be used as variations are listed at the end of the recipe.

1 *pound cabbage (use white part only)*
2 *tablespoons salt*
4 *cups cold water*
½ *teaspoon Szechuan peppercorns (optional)*
4 *dried red peppers or ½ teaspoon crushed red pepper*

Preparation:
Cut the white part of the cabbage into 1½ × 1-inch pieces and separate the leaves (you should have about 6 cups). Discard the green outer layers.

In a 2-quart wide-mouth jar, dissolve the salt in the water. Add the peppercorns and red peppers. Mix well, then add the cabbage, and press it down to the bottom within the liquid. It should be submerged under brine all the time. Cover and keep the jar at room temperature for 1 day, then in the refrigerator for about 3 to 4 days. Remove the cabbage from the liquid and serve cold. Use only clean, dry chopsticks or a fork to take out the cabbage.

Store the relish in the refrigerator. You may continue to use the brine. Add more fresh cabbage as a batch of relish is used up. Add about 2 teaspoons salt each time you add 6 cups cut-up fresh cabbage. Cabbage soaked in aged brine will be pickled in 2 to 3 days. After adding fresh cabbage two times, replace the peppers. When the liquid gets too sour or is no longer enough, it is time to add another recipe of freshly made brine.

Yield: 6 to 8 servings.

Choice of vegetables: Cut-up cauliflower, broccoli stems (remove the tough outer layers), white turnips (do not remove the skins, just scrape), young green beans, carrots (peeled), or young gingerroot may be used instead of cabbage or combined with it in the same jar. Two to 4 fresh chili peppers may be used instead of dried ones. Cut the fresh peppers without seeds into ¼-inch-wide strips.

Choice of seasonings: For a sweet-and-sour peppery seasoning, use in addition to the above ingredients 4 tablespoons distilled white vinegar, 6 tablespoons sugar, and 2 tablespoons salt. This brine can be used two times without adding any more seasonings.

Jo Pan Lou Sun

ASPARAGUS SALAD

> 1 *small bunch fresh asparagus (about 1 pound)*
> 1 *cup sliced carrots*

Dressing:
> 1 *tablespoon light or regular soy sauce*
> 1 *tablespoon sesame or corn oil*
> 1 *teaspoon salt*
> ½ *teaspoon sugar*
> ⅛ *teaspoon monosodium glutamate*

If an ingredient in the basic recipe is not readily available, or if an exotic variation is desired, see the list at the end of the recipe.

Preparation and cooking:
Peel each asparagus spear from the middle down to the white end. From the green tips down, start cutting the spears diagonally into ½-inch pieces. Continue cutting until the spears become too tough to cut, and discard the tough white ends.

Bring 1 quart water to a boil, then parboil the sliced carrots for 1 minute. Add the asparagus and continue to boil for 1 minute longer. Drain well and place in a salad bowl while still hot. Mix the dressing ingredients together, add to the bowl, and toss well. Serve hot. To serve cold, rinse the vegetables well with cold water, drain well, and add the dressing.

Yield: 4 servings.

Choice of vegetables or meat: If you wish to use watercress or spinach, parboil for 1 minute. Drain, rinse in cold water, squeeze to remove excess water, then chop finely. Add ¼ to ½ cup finely chopped water chestnuts, bamboo shoots, or cooked ham. Add the dressing and serve cold. If you wish to use broccoli stems, peel the tough outer layer of skin, slice, and parboil for 10 seconds. Rinse in cold water and drain. Serve cold with the dressing.

Liang Pan Sheng Ts'ai

CELERY AND RADISH SALAD

2 *cups each or a combination of celery, radishes,
and cucumber*

Dressing:
½ *teaspoon salt*
1 *tablespoon sugar*
1 *tablespoon light or regular soy sauce*
1 *tablespoon cider vinegar*
2 *teaspoons sesame or corn oil*

Preparation:
Peel off the outer layer of each stalk of celery. Break
into halves and pull off any tough veins. Wash and dry
well. Cut into ½-inch cubes.

Remove and discard the tops and roots of the radishes.
Wash and dry well. Lightly crush each radish with the
side of a large knife or cleaver.

Peel the cucumber and cut lengthwise in half. Remove
and discard any seeds from each cucumber half, then
cut crosswise into ¼-inch pieces.

Use 1 recipe of dressing for each 2 cups of any one or
any combination of the above vegetables. Toss and mix
well. Serve cold.

The radishes and celery can be prepared ahead of time;
they may be marinated for 4 to 24 hours and will taste
better that way.

Yield: 4 servings.

Choice of vegetables: You may use either lettuce or Belgian endive hearts. Blanched fresh bean sprouts, shredded zucchini, asparagus, or broccoli stems may also be used, cut into sections or slices.

Choice of seasonings: Add to the dressing ⅛ teaspoon ground red pepper or ¼ to ½ teaspoon Tabasco sauce.

Liang Pan Tou Chiao

GREEN BEAN SALAD WITH MUSTARD DRESSING

½ pound chicken livers

Marinade:
1 tablespoon cornstarch
1 tablespoon soy sauce
⅛ teaspoon monosodium glutamate

1 pound fresh green beans
2 teaspoons finely shredded fresh gingerroot
or ⅛ teaspoon white pepper

Mustard Dressing:
2 teaspoons mustard powder
1½ teaspoons cold water
1 teaspoon salt
1 teaspoon sugar
1 tablespoon soy sauce
1½ teaspoons cider vinegar
1 tablespoon sesame or corn oil

Preparation and cooking:
Slice the chicken livers lengthwise into ¼-inch-thick pieces. Add the marinade ingredients and mix well. Snap off and discard the ends of the green beans. Break the beans into 2-inch pieces (you should have about 4 cups). In a saucepan, bring 4 cups water to a boil. Add the beans and return to a boil. Cook for about 5 minutes, or until the beans are tender. Use a slotted spoon to remove the beans. Rinse with cold water and

141

drain. Dry the beans with paper towels and set aside along with the gingerroot. Bring the same water to a boil and blanch the marinated chicken livers for about 3 minutes, or until the livers are just firm. Drain and cool in a pot of cold water. Drain well again. Set in a salad bowl with the beans and the gingerroot.

To make the dressing, put the mustard powder in a mixing bowl with ½ teaspoon of the cold water and stir to form a thick paste and develop the hot mustard flavor. Gradually add the remaining cold water to make a smooth, thin paste. Add the remaining dressing ingredients. Pour the dressing over the beans and chicken livers and toss well. Chill in the refrigerator for 30 minutes and serve cold.

Yield: 4 servings.

Choice of other ingredients: Instead of chicken livers, you may use calf liver or pork kidney (inside cores removed), sliced and blanched without being marinated. Frozen green beans may be used instead of fresh, but omit the blanching. You may use only the green beans plus dressing, omitting the chicken livers.

Yen Huang Kua

SPICED PICKLED CUCUMBER

 4 *small pickling cucumbers*
 1 *clove garlic, minced*
 2 *teaspoons minced fresh gingerroot*
 ¼ *teaspoon crushed red pepper*
 2 *teaspoons salt*
1½ *tablespoons sugar*
 2 *tablespoons cider vinegar*
 ½ *teaspoon sesame or corn oil*

Preparation:
Wash and dry the cucumbers. Cut each into small, fingerlike rectangular pieces. You should have about 2 cups. Set aside.

Put the garlic, gingerroot, crushed red pepper, salt, sugar, vinegar, and cucumber pieces into a wide-mouth jar. Cover and shake well. Marinate for at least 4 hours. Dish out onto a serving plate and sprinkle with sesame oil. Serve as a small dish.

Yield: 1½ cups. 4 servings.

Choice of vegetable: 2 cups scraped Chinese white turnip or peeled kohlrabi may be used instead of cucumber; cut with grain into small, fingerlike pieces. Four cups of shredded Chinese celery cabbage may also be used. Combine with marinade ingredients and then weigh down with a heavy object for a few hours. Transfer to a jar.

Choice of seasoning: For a milder pickle, omit the garlic, gingerroot, and pepper.

Pong Pong Chi

PONG PONG CHICKEN

>   2 *cups boiled chicken*
>   2 *cups fresh mung bean sprouts*
>   2 *tablespoons finely shredded carrots*

Dressing:
>   2 *tablespoons peanut butter, diluted with*
>   *3 tablespoons warm water to make a smooth, thin*
>   *sauce*
>   ½ *teaspoon salt*
>   1 *tablespoon sugar*
>   ¼ *teaspoon monosodium glutamate*
>   2 *tablespoons soy sauce*
>   1 *tablespoon cider vinegar*
>   2 *tablespoons sesame or corn oil*
>   1 *teaspoon red pepper oil or Tabasco sauce, or to*
>   *taste*
>   2 *cloves garlic, finely chopped*
>   2 *tablespoons finely chopped scallion*

If an ingredient in the basic recipe is not readily available, or if an exotic variation is desired, see the list at the end of the recipe.

Preparation and cooking:
Use your fingers to tear the cooked chicken into very small strips (larger than shreds). Mix the bean sprouts and carrots together and blanch in boiling water for 10 seconds. Drain and rinse in cold water. Drain and dry well. Spread the bean sprouts and carrots on a serving

plate. Place the chicken on top in the center. This may be covered and kept in the refrigerator and taken out 30 minutes before serving.

Mix all the dressing ingredients together, except the garlic and scallion, into a very smooth sauce. Add the finely chopped garlic and scallion just before serving. The dressing without garlic and scallion can be made ahead of time and kept in the refrigerator for up to 1 week.

Drip the dressing over the chicken and vegetables and serve cold as a first course, along with other hot dishes, or as a one-dish meal with cold noodles or hot rice.

Yield: 4 servings.

Choice of meat: Roasted chicken, turkey, pork, cooked duck, or shrimp may be used instead of boiled chicken.

Choice of vegetables: Shredded lettuce, radishes, cucumbers, or soaked mung bean sheets may be used instead of bean sprouts and carrots.

Ching Ch'ieh Tzu

STEAMED EGGPLANT

During the late summer season eggplants are especially good. There is no need to peel the skin off, because it is tender and has a chewy texture. This dish can be prepared ahead of time and served cold. It is perfect to serve along with hot dishes.

   1 *medium eggplant (about 1 pound)*

Dressing:
   1½ *teaspoons sugar*
   ¼ *teaspoon ground red pepper, or to taste*
   1½ *teaspoons soy sauce*
   1 *tablespoon cider vinegar*
   1½ *tablespoons sesame or corn oil*

Preparation and cooking:
Wash the eggplant and remove and discard the stem. Cut lengthwise into 8 pieces. Lay the eggplant in a deep heatproof dish or a glass pie plate and steam for 20 minutes over high heat, or until soft. Turn off the heat and let the covered steamer stand for 10 minutes. Remove the eggplant dish and pour off the liquid that has accumulated during the steaming. Use chopsticks or a fork to separate the eggplant into 1 × 3-inch-long strips. Remove any hard seeds and tough pith. Mix the sauce ingredients well and pour over the eggplant. Serve either hot or cold.

Yield: 4 servings.

Rice Dishes and Tien Hsin

NAME OF DISH	NATURE OF DISH	PAGE
Ch'a Shao Pao Baked Roast Pork Buns	Chinese roast pork filling baked with rich bread dough.	166
Chiao-tzu Meat Dumplings	Cold-water dough; mixing and kneading is the key to obtaining the right consistency.	168
Shui Chiao Boiled Meat Dumplings	The meat and vegetable dumpling cooked in boiling water is a staple food of the northern region.	170
Cheng Chiao Steamed Meat Dumplings	Hot water is used in the dough. Cooked in a bamboo steamer, they are more delicate and elegant.	171
Kuo T'ieh Fried Meat Dumplings	Pan-fried meat dumpling, browned on one side.	171
Pao Ping Mandarin Pancakes	Homemade pancakes are far better than store-bought. They can be made ahead of time.	172

Rice is a primary food in the Chinese diet. Although supplemented by wheat and other grains in northern, colder sections of China, where rice is not easy to grow, its importance is nevertheless obvious. In fact, the Chinese word for rice, *fan*, is also the word used for "meal."

Many Chinese foods are specifically flavored to be compatible with rice and in fact to encourage increased consumption of rice. These dishes are called "rice-sending" dishes, and they refer to highly seasoned and relatively salty foods. Typical examples of such dishes are red-cooked foods and the salty foods from the Ningpo area.

Cooked rice is never thrown away, and in fact, there is ample opportunity to take advantage of leftover rice.

The simplest way of using it is to reheat it by steaming or adding water to it and boiling until soft. Another way to use it is in fried rice, which is a quick and easy-to-prepare one-dish meal that makes good use of other leftovers you may have. Best of all, it is delicious.

One of the most common ways to use rice, at least in the true Chinese home, is not very elegant but it offers a unique blend of tastes. Simply combine cooked rice with leftover meats and their gravies, vegetables and their liquids, bean curd, or almost any other food that is cluttering the refrigerator (although sweet-and-sour foods are not recommended). Add broth or water to make a hearty soup, add salt to taste, and heat thoroughly. Though such a concoction may seem odd, it can be delicious, satisfying, and unique every time you make it.

Tien hsin (sometimes written *dim sum*) refers to a category of Chinese foods that can be enjoyed any time of day or night and are commonly eaten as a snack or light meal. The literal translation of *tien hsin* is "to dot the heart."

Comparable to Western appetizers, pastries, canapés, or desserts, *tien hsin* come in many varieties and can be either simple or very fancy. For the most part, they are not sweet but rather meat or vegetable based. Different regions of China use different fillings, wrappers, and cooking techniques. For example, the filling can be made from rice, beans, sweet potatoes, taro roots, lotus roots, seeds, nuts, diced fruit, and so on. The noodles and wrappers are made from different grains, and the fillings run the spectrum from sweet or salty beans and vegetables to meat and fish. Finally every cooking method is employed: baking, steaming, stewing, and pan or deep frying.

Shan Yü Jou Ping

MEAT-FILLED POTATO BUNS

4 to 6 medium baking potatoes (about 1½ pounds)

Filling:
¼ pound ground lean beef (about ½ cup)
1 teaspoon cornstarch
½ teaspoon sugar
2 teaspoons soy sauce

¼ cup plus 1 tablespoon peanut or corn oil
1½ tablespoons cornstarch
¼ cup grated carrots
1½ teaspoons salt
¼ teaspoon monosodium glutamate
2 tablespoons black or white sesame seeds

Preparation:
Peel the potatoes and cut them into chunks. Cover with water and cook for about 20 minutes, or until soft.

Combine the filling ingredients in a mixing bowl and mix them thoroughly. Heat a pan, add 1 tablespoon of the oil, and stir-fry the filling for 2 minutes. Remove and let cool.

Drain off the water from the cooked potatoes, making sure that there is no water remaining. Mash thoroughly and smoothly with cornstarch. Add the grated carrots, salt, monosodium glutamate, and mix some more. Di-

151

vide into 12 portions. Shape each portion into a small cup and fill each cup with 2 teaspoons of the meat mixture. Pinch the edges together to make a 2-inch-diameter flat round bun. Sprinkle some sesame seeds on both sides, pressing them in to make them stick.

Cooking:
Heat a large frying pan over medium-high heat until it is very hot. Add 2 more tablespoons of the oil, then fry 6 buns at a time for about 5 minutes on each side, or until a golden brown crust forms. Do not turn the buns until the brown crust forms. Serve hot.

The buns can be reheated in a 375° oven in about 5 minutes.

Yield: 12 buns. 6 servings.

Choice of filling: Ground veal or pork, or ½ cup finely chopped braised bamboo shoots and 1 cup finely chopped fresh mushrooms may be used instead of beef.

Pai Fan

PLAIN RICE

The following are two different methods of cooking plain Chinese rice. Only water and rice are used. The proportions of rice and water may vary, depending on the degree of moisture or dryness of the rice dictated by personal taste.

Chu Fan

BOILED RICE

>   2 *cups long-grain rice*
>   3 *cups water*

Preparation and cooking:
Wash and drain the rice several times. To a heavy saucepan with a tight-fitting lid add the washed rice and the water. Place the saucepan over medium heat and bring the rice to a boil. Boil for 3 to 4 minutes, or until all the water appears to be absorbed by the rice. Cover and turn the heat down to a low simmer. Cook for 20 minutes. Turn off the heat but do not remove the pot from the stove or lift the cover; let the rice steam for 10 minutes.

Fluff the rice with wet chopsticks. Serve in warm bowls. Rice can be kept hot in a covered casserole in the oven at 150° to 170° for up to 30 minutes without drying out.

Cheng Fan

STEAMED RICE

2 cups oval- or long-grain rice

Water: 2 cups for oval-grain rice; 2½ cups for
   long-grain rice

Preparation and cooking:
Wash and drain the rice several times. Put the washed
rice in a large heatproof bowl and add the amount of
water that is called for. Let the rice soak in the water
for 30 minutes.

Place the bowl with the rice and water on a rack in a
pot containing several inches of water. The water level
should reach about 1½ inches below the bowl's rim.
Cover the pot or wok. Bring the water to a boil and
steam the rice over medium heat for about 30 minutes,
or until soft. Fluff the rice with wet chopsticks and
serve in the same bowl. If the bowl has a cover, cover
the rice between servings.

Yield: 6 cups cooked rice. 4 to 6 servings.

*Steamed rice topped with marinated or preserved
meats*: After the rice has steamed for 10 minutes, or
until the rice has absorbed the excess water, the
following meats and chicken may be added to the
partially cooked rice: 4 or 5 pieces of marinated, uncooked Broiled Chicken with Ginger Sauce (page 98),
or 4 links Chinese sausages, or ¼ preserved pressed

duck, or 1 strip of preserved belly of pork. Continue steaming for 30 minutes; the tasty juice of the meat soaks into the rice at the same time rice and meat are cooking. Cut the meat and serve with the rice. A very tasty one-dish meal.

How to reheat leftover rice: Leftover rice can be kept in a covered container in the refrigerator for 1 week to 10 days, or in the freezer for weeks. Leftover boiled or steamed rice can be heated in the steamer; place the cold rice in a rice bowl, sprinkle some water on before steaming. Or you can leave the leftover rice in the pot. Add some water, bring to a boil, then cook over low heat for about 15 minutes. It is also excellent to use for fried rice with or without egg.

Tan Ch'ao Fan

EGG-FRIED RICE

> 3 cups cold cooked rice *(separate the grains when rice is cold)*
> 2 *large eggs*
> 1 *teaspoon salt*
> 3 *tablespoons peanut or corn oil*
> 2 *scallions, chopped*
> 1½ *tablespoons soy sauce*

Preparation and cooking:
Put the rice in a mixing bowl, add the eggs and salt, and mix well. Heat a pan or wok until hot. Add the oil and scallions and stir-fry for a few seconds, then add the rice-and-egg mixture. With a spatula turn and stir until the eggs in the rice are cooked. Add the soy sauce and mix well. Serve hot.

If you intend to add leftover cooked meat or seafood, such as ham, chicken, turkey, roast pork, shrimp, or lobster, use about 1 cup diced meat of any kind or a combination of two kinds of meat and seafood, along with ½ cup vegetables, such as cooked peas or green beans or raw chopped lettuce or bean sprouts. Add the meat, seafood, and vegetables to the rice after you add the soy sauce. Make sure they are thoroughly heated. Add more salt to taste.

For an exotic flavor: Add 2 tablespoons oyster sauce instead of soy sauce. You may use chopped cooked Smithfield ham instead of other meat, but reduce the salt.

Chih Ma Ping

SESAME PINGS

     1 *package dry yeast*
    1½ *cups lukewarm water*
     2 *teaspoons sugar*
     4 *cups all-purpose flour (approximately)*
     ½ *pound bacon*
     1 *cup chopped scallions*
     ¼ *cup peanut or corn oil or shortening*
     2 *teaspoons salt*
     ¼ *cup white sesame seeds*

Preparation and cooking:
Sprinkle the yeast over the lukewarm water. Add the sugar and let it sit in a warm place for 2 minutes. Place the flour in a large mixing bowl. Add the dissolved yeast mixture to make a soft but not sticky dough and knead it until it feels smooth. Put the dough back into the bowl, cover with a lid or damp cloth, and let rise in a warm place for 30 minutes.

Cut the bacon into ¼-inch-size pieces. Fry them until most of the fat has left the meat but the bacon is still soft. Drain (you should have about ½ cup fried bacon) and save the fat for future use. Mix the cooked bacon with the scallions.

After the dough has risen, take ½ of it out and knead it into a soft dough. Roll out onto an 8 × 14-inch rectangle. Brush 1 tablespoon of the oil on the dough, then sprinkle on 1 teaspoon of the salt. Evenly distribute half of the scallions and bacon mixture over the dough. Roll the dough up lengthwise. Break or cut the roll into 10 pieces. Pinch each piece at both ends to seal in the filling. Lay each piece with the pinched side down, then roll each one out into a ¼-inch-thick, 3-inch-in-diameter circle. Brush each *ping* with water, then sprinkle with sesame seeds.

Heat 2 large frying pans over medium-high heat. Add 1 tablespoon oil to each pan. Place the *ping*, sesame-seed-side down, in the pan. Cover and cook for about 4 minutes. Turn over and cook 4 minutes more. Repeat the above procedure with the remaining dough. Serve hot. The *pings* can be reheated in a toaster oven.

Yield: 20 *pings*. 10 servings for breakfast or lunch.

Choice of filling: You may use ½ cup chopped cooked ham (half lean, half fat) instead of bacon. Or only scallions may be used, without meat, but increase the shortening to 6 tablespoons and the salt to 4 teaspoons.

Liang Pan Mien

NOODLE SALAD

This is a one-dish meal that offers an opportunity to use interesting serving accessories. It lends itself to picnics as well as home luncheons. It consists of cold egg noodles, finely shredded meat, and mixed vegetables, with a tasty peanut butter and pepper sauce. The meat and vegetables may be arranged on a platter or tray and the noodles in a salad bowl. Each person receives a soup or salad bowl with about a cupful of noodles, mixes his own sauce, and adds any other ingredients he wishes. Chinese cooks prefer to buy fresh egg noodles at Oriental food stores, but very thin spaghetti may be used instead.

Dressing:
- 6 *tablespoons creamy peanut butter*
- 6 *tablespoons warm water*
- ¼ *cup soy sauce*
- 2 *tablespoons cider vinegar*
- ¼ *cup sesame or corn oil*
- 2 *teaspoons red pepper oil or 1 teaspoon ground red pepper with 2 teaspoons oil*
- 4 *teaspoons sugar*
- 1 *teaspoon salt*
- ½ *teaspoon monosodium glutamate*

- 1 *pound fresh egg noodles or ¾ pound very thin spaghetti*
- 2 *tablespoons sesame or corn oil*
- 1 *tablespoon soy sauce*

Preparation and cooking:
Combine the peanut butter with the warm water to make a smooth, thin sauce. Add the remaining dressing ingredients to make a very smooth dressing. The dressing can be made ahead of time and stored in a jar in the refrigerator for many weeks. It is also very good for hot noodles.

Drop the egg noodles into 3 to 4 quarts boiling water and stir to separate them. Boil for about 3 to 4 minutes; the noodles should not be too soft. Rinse under cold water and drain thoroughly.

Spread the noodles to dry for 10 minutes. Add the oil and soy sauce to the noodles and toss well. Cover and chill in the refrigerator for no more than 2 hours.

Suggested cooked meat and raw vegetables: 2 to 3 cups shredded roast pork, boiled chicken, turkey, duck, or ham; shredded Egg Crêpes (recipe below); 4 to 6 cups shredded cucumbers, radishes, lettuce, or bean sprouts; minced scallions and garlic.

EGG CRÊPES

Beat 2 eggs thoroughly with a pinch of salt and set aside for 10 minutes. Heat an 8-inch skillet until very hot. Turn the heat down to low and let the pan cool off. Lightly grease the pan. Pour in ¼ of the beaten eggs and tip the pan around so that the egg spreads into a thin, even layer in the pan. Cook over low heat until the egg coagulates. Lift up, flip over, and let cook briefly on the other side. Repeat the procedure to make 3 more crêpes. Let cool, then shred into very fine 2-inch-long strips.

Choice of sauce: For a mild sauce, combine the following ingredients:

¼ cup soy sauce
¼ cup wine vinegar
2 tablespoons sesame or corn oil
2 teaspoons sugar
¼ teaspoon monosodium glutamate

Mix well and serve in a sauceboat.

Liang Mien Huang

TWO-SIDES BROWNED NOODLES

In this dish a bed of noodles is browned in a frying pan or wok. The resulting thin, cakelike noodle patty is brown and has a crunchy burnt crust on both sides but is still soft inside. The other ingredients and the sauce are poured on top of the noodles but not mixed in when served. Thus, one can taste the different flavor of each ingredient, with just enough sauce absorbed by the noodles.

- ½ pound lean pork, shredded (about 1 cup)
- 2 tablespoons soy sauce
- 2 teaspoons cornstarch
- ½ pound raw shrimp, shelled, deveined, and chopped
- ½ teaspoon salt
- 3 cups finely shredded cabbage
- ¼ cup finely shredded carrots
- 2 Egg Crêpes, shredded (page 161)
- 2 scallions, white part only, shredded

- 1 pound fresh egg noodles
- 8 tablespoons peanut or corn oil

Sauce:
- ¾ cup chicken broth
- 1½ tablespoons soy sauce
- 1½ teaspoons cornstarch

If an ingredient in the basic recipe is not readily available, or if an exotic variation is desired, see the list at the end of the recipe.

Preparation:
Mix the pork with 1 tablespoon of the soy sauce and 1 teaspoon of the cornstarch. In a separate bowl, mix the shrimp with ½ teaspoon salt and the remaining 1 teaspoon cornstarch. Set aside.

Place the shredded cabbage, carrots, Egg Crêpes, and scallions on a large plate.

Cook the egg noodles in 3 quarts boiling water for 2 to 3 minutes. Rinse under cold water. Drain. Mix the remaining 1 tablespoon soy sauce with the noodles and set aside.

Cooking:
Heat a large skillet or wok over medium heat until very hot. Add 1 tablespoon of the oil to coat the pan. Spread the cooked noodles in the skillet and cook without stirring for about 5 minutes. The noodles will start to brown and burn a little. Add 1 tablespoon of the oil to the side of the pan, then flip over the browned noodle patty and brown the other side in the same manner. Transfer to a large platter and keep warm in the oven.

Separately stir-fry the pork and shrimp with 2 tablespoons of the oil. Set on the same plate as each item is cooked. Add the remaining 2 tablespoons oil to the same pan and stir-fry the cabbage and carrots for 2 minutes. Return the cooked pork and shrimp to the pan and stir with the vegetables to heat through.

Mix the sauce ingredients together very well, then pour them into the pan with the meat and vegetables, stirring to mix well. Cook until a light glaze coats the ingredients. Pour the entire contents of the pan on top of the hot noodle patty. Garnish with shredded Egg Crêpes and scallions. Serve hot as a wonderful one-dish luncheon meal with hot tea.

Yield: 6 servings.

Choice of meat: Instead of pork, you may use boneless, skinless chicken breast, shredded with the grain, or flank or strip steak, shredded with the grain or sliced against the grain.

Choice of vegetable and exotic ingredients: Instead of shredded carrots, you may use 1 cup sliced fresh mushrooms or 6 presoaked dried Chinese black mushrooms and ½ cup shredded bamboo shoots.

Ch'a Shao Pao

BAKED ROAST PORK BUNS

Dough:
- 1 package dry yeast
- ¾ cup warm water
- ⅓ cup sugar
- 2 large eggs plus 1 egg, well beaten
- ½ cup sweet butter or margarine
- ½ teaspoon salt
- 4 cups all-purpose flour (approximately)

Filling:
- 1 cup chopped yellow onion
- 2 tablespoons peanut or corn oil
- 2 cups chopped Chinese Roast Pork (page 100)
- ¼ cup water
- ½ teaspoon salt
- 2 tablespoons sugar
- 2 tablespoons soy sauce
- 1 tablespoon dry sherry
- ⅛ teaspoon ground black pepper
- ¼ teaspoon monosodium glutamate
- 2 tablespoons cornstarch combined with ¼ cup water
- ¼ cup chopped scallions

Preparation and cooking:
Sprinkle the dry yeast over the warm water. Add 1 tablespoon sugar and stir. Set aside. In a mixing bowl, cream the butter with the remaining sugar. Add the yeast mixture, the salt, and enough flour to make a soft

dough. Add 2 of the eggs, more flour, and knead until the dough looks smooth. Cover the bowl with a dry cloth and let rise in a warm place for 1½ hours, or until the dough doubles in volume.

In the meantime make the filling: Stir-fry the chopped onion in the oil. Add the pork, then the water. Next add the salt, sugar, soy sauce, sherry, pepper, and monosodium glutamate. Stir the cornstarch-and-water combination and add to the pork filling. Add the chopped scallions. Stir briefly. Let cool completely and use as the filling for the buns.

Punch down the dough, which has risen, and knead it a little. Cut it into 20 pieces and shape them into balls. With your hand, flatten each into a 3-inch disk. Put about 2 tablespoons of the filling in the center of each disk. Pinch the edges of the disk, gathering them together to seal. Put each finished bun seal-side down on an oiled baking sheet. Let rise again for 20 to 30 minutes. Glaze with beaten egg and bake in a preheated 350° oven for 20 minutes. The buns can be reheated in a 350° oven for 10 minutes. Serve hot.

Yield: 20 buns. 10 servings for a lunch or light supper.

Chiao-tzu

MEAT DUMPLINGS

Filling:
- 1 pound ground pork or beef
- 1 teaspoon salt
- 2 tablespoons soy sauce
- 1 tablespoon sesame or corn oil
- 4 tablespoons chicken broth
- ½ cup chopped cooked vegetables, such as celery cabbage, carrots, spinach, or green beans

Wrappers:*
- 2 cups all-purpose flour
- ¾ cup cold water (use hot water for steamed dumplings)

Preparation:

In a mixing bowl, combine the filling ingredients, except the vegetables, and stir the mixture with a spoon in one direction only. Add the chopped vegetables and mix some more. Keep the filling in the refrigerator while you are making the wrappers.

To make the wrappers, put the flour into a large bowl and make a well in the center. Gradually add the water and, with your fingers, stir to make a firm dough. (It is important to start with a firm dough; more water can

*Ready-made wrappers, purchased in Chinese or Japanese food stores, may be used. They can be kept in the freezer until you are ready to use them. Thaw wrappers, put the filling in the center, then apply cold water to the edge to ease sealing.

be gradually added to make a softer dough.) Knead until the dough is soft and smooth. Return the dough to the bowl and cover with a damp cloth to keep the dough moist. Let stand for about 15 minutes. The dough can be made ahead of time and kept in a tightly covered container in the refrigerator for up to 2 days.

Turn the dough onto a lightly floured surface and knead for 5 minutes. Divide it into 2 parts. Keep ½ covered in the bowl while you shape the other half into a cylinder about 10 inches long and 1 inch in diameter. Cut into 15 pieces. Lay the pieces cut-side down and dust them lightly with flour. Press each piece with the palm of your hand to flatten it to a ¼-inch thickness. Use a small rolling pin to roll each piece into a 2½-inch-diameter disk about ⅛ inch thick. Turn counterclockwise a quarter turn as you roll to keep the shape round and the edges thinner than the center. Cover the finished wrapper with a dry cloth to prevent the dumplings from drying out.

Put about 1 tablespoon of the filling in the center of each wrapper. Fold the dough in half to cover the filling. Starting from one end, pinch the edge of the dough, and with the fingers of the other hand, push the extra dough around to the front so that pleats form on the center front. Use your thumb and forefinger to press and seal the openings. Arrange the meat dumplings on a floured tray and cover with a dry cloth. Repeat the procedure with the remaining dough. The meat dumplings can be frozen on the tray, then transferred to a container. They will keep in the freezer for several weeks.

The ready-made wrappers can be kept in the freezer until you are ready to use them. Thaw the wrappers and put the filling in the center, then apply some cold water to the edge to ease sealing.

Yield: 30 *chiao-tzu.*

Now the *chiao-tzu* are ready to be boiled, steamed, or fried. Because the methods of cooking are different, each one has its own name.

Yield: 4 servings for a lunch or light dinner.

Shui Chiao

BOILED MEAT DUMPLINGS

In a large pot bring 2 quarts water to a rolling boil. Add about 30 dumplings and stir once. Cover and return to a boil. Add 1 cup cold water, cover, and wait until the water boils again. Repeat the cold-water treatment twice more. Then, cover the pot and let the dumplings sit for 5 minutes more. Remove the meat dumplings with a strainer. Serve hot with a dip of 3 tablespoons wine vinegar, 2 teaspoons soy sauce, and 1 cup hot, boiling dumpling water (the water used to cook the dumplings). The liquid can also be used as a beverage, served to each person along with the dumplings.

Cheng Chiao

STEAMED MEAT DUMPLINGS

Oil the steamer rack or a plate and place the finished dumplings directly on it, each ½ inch apart. Cover and steam over medium-high heat for 15 minutes. Serve immediately either in the steamer or on the plate.

When properly made, steamed meat dumplings should have a lot of juice. The best way to eat them is to use your fingers to lift one by the top and immediately transfer it to a spoon, so that when you bite into the delicious steamed dumpling, no sauce is lost.

Kuo T'ieh

FRIED MEAT DUMPLINGS

Place 1 large or 2 small frying pans over medium heat until very hot. Remove the frying pans from the heat and add ½ tablespoon oil to coat each pan. Arrange the uncooked dumplings one against the other in a circle. Return the frying pan to the heat and fry the dumplings until the bottoms turn light brown. Add 1 cup water, cover, and cook over medium-high heat until the water has evaporated. This takes about 8 to 10 minutes. Uncover, add 1½ tablespoons oil around the sides, and let the dumplings fry some more until a dark brown crust forms on the bottom. Carefully free the sides and loosen the dumplings from the pan. Serve hot, brownside up. Use wine vinegar combined with a few drops of Tabasco sauce as a dip.

Pao Ping

MANDARIN PANCAKES

2 *cups all-purpose flour*
⅞ *cup boiling water*
1 *tablespoon peanut or corn oil*

Preparation and cooking:
Place the flour in a large bowl and gradually pour in the boiling water while stirring with chopsticks or a fork. Add 1 teaspoon of the oil, stir in, then knead with the dry flour around the bowl until it is soft and smooth. (Add more flour if it is too sticky.) Cover the dough in the bowl with a damp cloth and let it sit for 15 minutes.

Knead the dough again and divide into 2 portions. Keep 1 covered in the bowl and roll the other out evenly ⅕-inch thick. Using a round cookie cutter, cut out pancakes 2 inches in diameter. Cover the cut-out pancakes with a cloth while you are working with the rest of the dough. Knead the scraps into the remaining ½ of the dough and continue rolling out and cutting more pancakes. The total number of pancakes should be about 26 to 28. Lightly and evenly brush oil on one side of half the pancakes. Place an unoiled pancake on top of each oiled one. Roll each double pancake out on both sides, working from the center out, to about 6 to 7 inches in diameter.

Heat a frying pan over medium heat until it is hot. Fry each pancake without oil until it begins to bubble, then turn it over. This takes less than 1 minute on each side. Remove the double pancakes from the pan and pull the 2 pancakes apart while still hot. Stack the thin pancakes while you cook the rest. Keep the finished pancakes covered with a damp cloth.

If wrapped in foil, the pancakes can be frozen for future use. Before serving, heat the pancakes in a covered steamer or a colander placed in a covered pan of boiling water for 10 minutes, or until the pancakes are hot and pliable.

Yield: 26 to 28 pancakes.

Index